LAUBACH WAY TO
ENGLISH

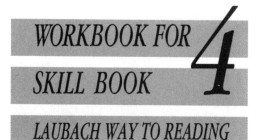

WORKBOOK FOR **4**

SKILL BOOK

LAUBACH WAY TO READING

Jeanette D. Macero

ISBN 0-88336-374-7

© 1987, 1991 new cover art

 New Readers Press
Publishing Division of
Laubach Literacy
1320 Jamesville Ave., Syracuse, New York 13210

Printed in the United States of America

Edited by Kay Koschnick

Designed by Chris Steenwerth

20 19 18 17 16 15 14 13 12 11
10

To Daniel J. Macero with appreciation for his creative suggestions and constant encouragement to me in writing LWE Workbooks 1-4.

Table of Contents

To the Teacher

This *Workbook for Skill Book 4* is designed to give students additional practice in listening to, speaking, reading, and writing the patterns of English presented in *Skill Book 4*. The vocabulary is controlled to the reading vocabulary taught at each lesson level in *Skill Book 4*, although some new words are introduced.

The workbook gives practice in 19 skill areas that are important in mastering English. (See the chart titled "The Workbook at a Glance" below.) There are exercises on the use of nouns, pronouns, articles, prepositions, modifiers, and coordinating conjunctions. Students have opportunities to practice verb tenses and to make and answer questions in the affirmative and negative. They practice writing sentences by completing sentences, by writing original sentences, and by combining two sentences into one. There are also practical tasks like writing notes and want ads, reading a map and a pie chart, and filling out forms.

A major type of exercise in the workbook is the cloze exercise, here titled "Story with Missing Words." These exercises are passages from *Skill Book 4* stories in which every nth word (from 5th to 9th) is left blank, except for names or numbers that would be impossible to figure out from context. Any appropriate word—that is, any word that is both grammatically correct and logical—is acceptable as an answer. In this type of exercise, the student is required to integrate *all* of his language skills. Cloze exercises are thus significantly different from exercises that focus on only one skill at a time.

Listening exercises are included to sharpen the students' ability to hear the difference between pronoun forms, verb endings, and contractions that are often difficult for students to differentiate. Students are also asked to listen and write what they hear.

An answer key is provided at the back of the book. Students should be discouraged from looking at the answers while they are doing the exercises. At times, you may allow students to check their own work, but *you* should check their work as much as possible so that you can help them understand and correct their errors. Also, your judgment is needed in cases where more than one answer is possible. Be sure to praise students for their correct answers. If a student gives correct answers that are not shown in the key, praise him for showing knowledge of the language beyond that expected or already taught.

How to Use the Exercises

The exercises for each lesson are arranged in increasing order of difficulty. Some exercise pages have a note at the bottom that gives specific instructions to the teacher. In general, however, the following steps are useful for the majority of the exercises.

1. Teach any new words listed at the top of the page. Students should be able to sound out most of the new words; phonetic respellings are provided where necessary. If a word is marked with an asterisk, however, tell the students what the word is. The asterisk indicates a sight word containing a sound or spelling not yet taught.

2. Read the directions orally with the students. Never assign an exercise without being sure that the students know what is required in it.

3. In each exercise, go over the first item for which the answer is supplied. Ask the students to do the rest of the exercise on their own. Then check their work. Praise them if the exercise is correctly done. If a student's answer is incorrect, explain the error. Have the student write the correct answer and then read it aloud. If, after doing the example, a student still cannot do the exercise, go over the example again. If necessary, do one or two additional items of the actual exercise with the student. In some cases, it may be necessary to review briefly the grammatical item of the exercise causing difficulty.

4. Have the students follow the directions carefully and keep the sentences in the tenses given.

5. Most exercises for a particular lesson can be assigned as homework, along with the homework for that lesson in *Skill Book 4*.

Tips on Specific Types of Exercises

Cloze exercises. In the "Story with Missing Words," the students are to fill in *one* word in each blank. Encourage them to search for context clues that will help them figure out the word to write. Have the students both look back and read ahead to find clues. Teach them how to figure out what words are appropriate for any given blank. In the cloze exercise "A Family Reunion" in Lesson 2, there is the sentence: *My brother and his wife came from Texas with their little _____.* By reading ahead in the paragraph, the students find the word *She,* which tells them they must supply the word *girl* and not *boy.*

If a cloze exercise is done in class, there is no time limit for finishing it. After the students have completed a story, go over it and explain any errors.

If a cloze exercise is done as homework, students may check their answers against the corresponding passage in *Skill Book 4.* You should also look over the students' completed passages. For one thing, you can judge whether their answers are acceptable when they have not used the exact word given in the skill book. (In Lesson 8, for example, there is this sentence: *Jake Bush lived in a one-room cabin _____ a beautiful brook.* Although the skill book uses the word *near,* the word *beside* would also be acceptable.) Also, you will want to see what kinds of errors the students are making, such as errors with verb forms, prepositions, or articles. Then you can consult the "Workbook at a Glance" to find exercises in the students' specific problem areas.

Error correction. Students are asked to find and correct the errors in the sentences. The errors are those typically made by non-native speakers of English. In contrast to most other exercises, error correction exercises contain many different problems. They are useful as review.

Word order. Stress the importance of word order in English, but do not go into detail about possible variations of word order. It is best in declarative sentences to stress this order: subject, verb, object(s), place, and time.

Verb tenses. Point out the words (for example *girl, girls; since, for*) that indicate the form of the verb to be used. Also point out the necessary sequence of tenses in sentences. In the sentence *She worked until she (became) tired,* the use of *worked* in the first clause requires the use of *became* in the second clause.

Writing sentences. Go over the original sentences the students write. Check for errors, and explain in simple terms anything that is wrong with the sentences. Praise the students for whatever they can write correctly. If the students cannot write sentences on their own, do some sample sentences orally. Have the students write these sentences. Then reassign the exercises for homework, asking the students to write different sentences.

Listening exercises. Unlike other exercises these must be done in class. Do the examples with the students, repeating them if necessary. Read the sentences in a natural manner at a regular pace. Do not emphasize the items being taught or enunciate the words with extra care.

If students have difficulty with a listening exercise, do it again. If the exercise allows, give different answers the second time.

How to Vary the Exercises

While most of the exercises were designed primarily to be used as homework, they may also be used to advantage in class or while tutoring.

1. Some of the exercises may be done orally with books closed. Help the students with their pronunciation and intonation at this time.

2. Have the students do the exercises as homework. Then, at the next class session, have them read the answers to you. Listen for pronunciation and intonation errors. Have students imitate your pronunciation of words, phrases and sentences that cause them difficulty. In a class situation, students can work in pairs with one student asking questions (for example) and the other answering them.

3. Some exercises can be used for dictation—for example, the sentence order exercises, the completed "Stories with Missing Words," and any verb form exercise. First, read the entire sentence at a normal pace; do not enunciate in an exaggerated manner. Next, dictate the sentence in meaningful segments, reading each segment twice.

If dictation is still difficult for students, the sentences can be read in segments. *Some computers / do / just / one job* can be read in the segments marked by the slashes. As students become more proficient with dictation, the

segments can be longer and can be read once instead of twice. For example: *Some computers do / just one job.*

Give the students time to look over what they have written. Read the sentence again at a normal pace so students can check any parts they have doubts about.

Finally, have the students correct their sentences according to the model in the workbook. If they make their corrections in a different color, you can easily see what mistakes they are making. It is important for you to look over the dictation. The errors will give you invaluable insight into the students' learning processes and show you where the students need more practice.

The Workbook at a Glance

Skill areas	Lesson and practice numbers
Nouns and pronouns	1-1, 2-5, 3-1, 3-6, 6-1, 9-5, 13-1, 16-1, 17-5, 21-4, 22-1
Verbs, tenses	1-5, 1-6, 2-3, 2-4, 3-2, 7-1, 8-6, 10-3, 11-4, 13-2, 14-2, 15-1, 15-2, 15-5, 19-7, 22-3
Prepositions	1-2, 3-5, 5-1, 9-1, 9-2, 13-4, 18-2, 20-2
Articles, modifiers	2-1, 2-2, 5-3, 8-1, 11-5, 11-6, 12-1, 15-3, 16-1, 16-2, 21-4
Subordinate conjunctions	8-2, 9-2, 19-5
Homonyms	7-2, 21-7, 22-2
Make questions	1-7, 3-4, 7-3, 8-5, 11-1, 12-6, 14-1, 14-5, 17-3, 21-3, 21-5
Answer questions	2-7, 11-3, 12-3, 12-4, 12-5, 13-3, 17-1, 17-4, 20-4, 21-3, 23-1
Make negative sentences	4-3, 4-4, 14-1, 14-3, 15-4
Word order in sentences	1-3, 3-3, 4-5, 6-2, 7-5, 8-4, 9-4, 18-1, 21-6, 22-4, 23-5
Sentence order	8-3, 13-6, 22-6, 23-2
Make new words	2-1, 2-2, 15-3, 16-1, 16-2, 17-5, 21-4, 22-1
Alphabetical order	21-1, 21-2
Combine sentences	5-4, 6-3, 7-4, 7-6, 10-3, 10-5, 12-2, 14-4, 16-3, 16-4, 18-3, 19-2, 23-3
Correct the errors	17-2, 18-6, 19-6, 20-3, 22-5, 23-4
Write sentences	1-4, 1-6, 1-8, 1-9, 2-6, 4-1, 4-2, 4-6, 6-4, 6-5, 8-7, 9-6, 9-7, 9-8, 10-4, 10-7, 11-2, 11-7, 13-1, 14-3, 15-5, 18-1, 18-4, 18-5, 19-1, 19-3, 19-4, 19-7, 19-8, 20-1, 20-4, 21-6
Story with missing words	2-8, 4-7, 5-5, 6-6, 8-8, 10-8, 12-7, 16-6, 18-7, 23-7
Read and fill in forms	3-8, 5-2, 9-3, 10-1, 10-2, 10-6, 15-6, 16-5, 17-7, 20-4
Listen	3-7, 7-7, 9-9, 11-8, 13-5, 15-7, 17-6, 20-5, 21-8, 23-6

Lesson 1

PRACTICE 1: Singular and Plural Forms of Nouns

Write the singular or plural form of the missing noun.

1. Doctors do not have the cure for some (sickness) _sicknesses_____.

2. You use your Social Security number when you pay some (tax) _____.

3. Put an X in the two (box) _____.

4. I had two English (class) _____ today.

5. Most (business) _____ are not open on Sundays.

6. (Computer) _____ have become cheaper.

7. A computer is a (machine) _____ that works with facts like

   (name) _____ and (address) _____.

8. I'll have some (milk) _____.

PRACTICE 2: Prepositions

Write *at, in, into, of,* or *for*.

 1. This is the age __of___ the computer.

 2. A human must put facts _____ the machine.

 3. Computers are used _____ businesses.

 4. Doctors do not have a cure _____ some sicknesses.

 5. Computers help to teach many kinds _____ things.

 6. Some computer games can amuse you _____ home.

 7. Print a letter _____ each box.

 8. Computers help us _____ many ways.

 9. Some people are afraid _____ computers.

10. We live _____ a computer age.

11. Ann asked the computer _____ some facts.

12. You can learn with computers _____ class or _____ home.

PRACTICE 3: Word Order in Sentences

Add the words to the sentences.

1. (very) A computer can find answers quickly.

   A computer can find answers very quickly.

2. (much) This machine works faster than a human.

   _____

3. (other) They help to make paper, cars, TVs, and many things.

   _____

4. (quickly) Computers help you to telephone other places.

   _____

5. (own) You can play these games on your TV.

   _____

6. (just) Some computers do one job.

   _____

7. (as) It may be little as a radio.

   _____

8. (very) Computers tell us if a person is sick.

   _____

PRACTICE 4: Finish the Sentences

Read the words. Then finish the sentence.

1. Computers are so cheap that *many businesses use them.* .

2. Computers are so quick that _____ .

3. Some computers are so huge that _____ .

4. He drinks so much coffee that _____ .

5. It's snowing so hard that _____ .

6. Ed is so angry that _____ .

PRACTICE 5: Passive Verbs

Write the missing verb.

stolen used made
trained read dropped

1. Money can be (steal) _stolen_____.

2. Computers are (use) _____ to build airplanes.

3. People are (train) _____ to fly airplanes.

4. Computers can be (use) _____ to hurt us.

5. Some business forms can be (read) _____ by computers.

6. Bombs can be (make) _____ with the help of computers.

7. Bombs can be (drop) _____ with the help of computers.

8. People will be (train) _____ to use computers.

PRACTICE 6: The Passive

Read the words. Then finish the sentence.

1. A human must put *facts* into the computer.

   _Facts must be put into the computer._____

2. A person uses *computers* at home.

   Computers _____

3. People use *computers* to build airplanes.

   Computers _____

4. People can steal *money* from banks by computer.

   Money _____

5. Computers can read some *business forms*.

   Some business forms _____

6. People will use *computers* in businesses and at home.

   Computers _____

PRACTICE 7: Make Questions

Read the sentences. Write questions.

1. A human must put facts into the computer.

   Must a human put facts into the computer?

2. A person uses computers at home.

   _____

3. People can steal money from banks by computer.

   _____

   _____

4. Some computers do just one job.

   _____

5. People will use computers at home.

   _____

6. Carla had two English classes today.

   _____

7. Gail paid her telephone bill.

   _____

8. Gail's uncle was taking pictures at the wedding.

   _____

   _____

9. Miller is the man wearing the yellow shirt.

   _____

   _____

10. Jason has had lunch.

   _____

PRACTICE 8: Finish the Sentences

Read the words. Then finish the sentences.

1. Computers tell what _sickness a person has._

2. A computer can tell what _____

3. We understand what _____

4. The doctors know what _____

5. Some people understand what _____

6. Carla knows what _____

PRACTICE 9: Write Sentences

Write sentences with *may*.

1. _A computer may be huge or little._

2. _____

_____

3. _____

_____

4. _____

_____

5. _____

_____

6. _____

_____

PRACTICE 1: The Ending -est

Write the word. Add -est to make a new word.

1. young ___youngest___   7. high _____

2. good ___best___   8. light _____

3. fast _____   9. big _____

4. cheap _____   10. happy _____

5. sad _____   11. pretty _____

6. large _____   12. good _____

PRACTICE 2: Adjectives with -est

Use -est words in sentences.

1. I had potato salad, ham, and ribs. I liked the ribs ___best___.
   good

2. At 17, I am the _____ nephew in the family.
   young

3. Hugh acted the _____ to rescue his aunt.
   fast

4. Kay wants to buy the _____ dress she can find.
   cheap

5. Red is the _____ color.
   bright

6. She is the _____ doctor in the city.
   good

7. Ellen was the _____ person in the church.
   sad

8. This is the _____ computer I have ever seen.
   large

9. It is the _____ day of the year.
   hot

10. Carmen is the _____ woman in the class.
    pretty

PRACTICE 3: Past Tense

Write the past tense of the verb in the sentence.

1. We _____ _had_ _____ a family reunion last weekend.
       have

2. A few of my cousins _____ from Canada last week.
                          come

3. My aunt and uncle _____ a big barbecue for Saturday.
                        plan

4. She _____ with my father yesterday.
          argue

5. I _____ fishing with my cousins last weekend.
        go

6. Last year, many people _____ from choking.
                             die

7. Last night, Ed _____ when he _____ barbecued ribs.
                     choke   eat

8. I _____ my cousins some stories yesterday.
        tell

9. Jason _____ his leg last week.
            break

10. My aunt _____ the meat and the bread.
               cut

11. Kay _____ eggs for breakfast yesterday.
           eat

12. My aunt _____ dinner for everyone last night.
               make

PRACTICE 4: Present Perfect Tense

Write the sentences using *have* + the verb.

1. I _haven't seen_ so many of my relatives since 1985.

not, see

2. They _____ there since my grandfather retired.

live

3. My father _____ at the glass factory since he was a young man.

work

4. Ed _____ on York Street since he was 18.

live

5. I _____ computer games since I got my own computer.

play

6. Aunt Ellen _____ barbecued ribs since the meat stuck in her throat.

not, eat

7. I _____ anyone since the reunion when I rescued my niece.

not, rescue

8. People _____ computers since they learned how much they can do.

use

9. We _____ in Indian Valley for three years.

live

10. They _____ their car many miles since they got it.

drive

11. Gail _____ many thank you letters since her birthday.

write

12. I _____ Gail and Jason a wedding gift yet.

not, give

PRACTICE 5: *someone/anyone*

Read the sentence. Write *someone* or *anyone*.

1. I didn't think __*anyone*__ my age was going.

2. _____ told a family story.

3. We didn't see _____ in the water.

4. My father never argues with _____.

5. I was glad that _____ my age was at the reunion.

6. _____ must put facts into the computer.

PRACTICE 6: Finish the Sentences

A. Finish the sentences.

1. I'm glad that *he went to the reunion.*

2. My father is glad that _____

3. My mother is glad that _____

4. My teacher is glad that _____

5. My family is glad that _____

6. My friend is glad that _____

B. Write sentences. Tell what you are glad about.

1. *I'm glad that I went to the reunion.*

2. _____

3. _____

4. _____

5. _____

6. _____

PRACTICE 7: Answer Questions (Review)

Write a short answer to each question.

1. Do you play cards? No, *I don't.* ————————————

   Do you like to go camping? Yes, *I do.* ————————————

2. Is dinner ready? Yes, ————————————

3. Were you drinking beer? No, ————————————

4. Have you had lunch yet? No, ————————————

5. Do some computers do just one job? Yes, ————————————

6. Did Hugh act fast to rescue his aunt? Yes, ————————————

7. Can someone choke on a piece of meat? Yes, ————————————

8. Does Ed have enough money? No, ————————————

9. Is the teacher glad that you are learning English? Yes, ————————————

10. Will Hugh's family continue to have reunions? Yes, ————————————

11. Have the Oak family lived in Indian Valley for three years? No, ————————————

12. Are some people afraid of computers? Yes, ————————————

13. Will someone help Ellen? No, ————————————

14. Can anyone learn to swim? Yes, ————————————

15. Am I right? Yes, ————————————

16. Can computers think? No, ————————————

PRACTICE 8: Story with Missing Words

Write the missing words.

A Family Reunion

Last weekend, we had a family reunion. At first, I refused to go. _____ didn't think anyone my age was _____. But my mother felt hurt when _____ refused. So I went.

The reunion _____ at the home of my Aunt _____ and Uncle John. Aunt Mary is _____ mother's sister. At 17, I am _____ youngest nephew. This was a reunion _____ my mother's family.

Aunt Mary and _____ John have a big home on _____ Huron. Their home has a lovely _____ of Lake Huron. We live just _____ few miles from them. But we _____ have a view of Lake Huron.

_____ aunt and uncle were planning a _____ barbecue for Saturday. More than thirty _____ were coming. My parents and I _____ on Friday to help my aunt _____ uncle get ready.

On Saturday, relatives _____ from far and near. My grandmother _____ grandfather came from Florida. They have _____ there since my grandfather retired. Grandmother _____ me a big hug and kiss. _____ said, "Hugh, I haven't seen you _____ you were a boy. You have _____ a man!"

My brother and his _____ came from Texas with their little _____. I was glad to see my three-year-old _____ for the first time. She gave _____ a big hug and said, "I _____ my Uncle Hugh."

PRACTICE 1: Pronouns with *-self*

Answer the questions. Use *by* + *myself, himself,* or *herself.*

1. Do you live alone?

   Yes, *I live by myself.* _____

2. Does Kitty O'Toole live alone?

   No, _____

3. Does Hugh live alone?

   No, _____

4. Was Ed cleaning the kitchen alone?

   Yes, _____

5. Do you go to the English class alone?

   Yes, _____

6. Was Jane in the apartment alone?

   Yes, _____

PRACTICE 2: Verb Forms with *to* and without *to*

In each sentence, use the verb with *to* or the verb without *to.*

1. I need a roommate ___*to share*___ the rent.

share

2. We want you _____ at home.

live

3. She made me _____ her the answer.

give

4. Kitty liked _____.

swim

5. The Hoovers let Jane _____ one of their rugs.

take

6. Mrs. Oak went _____ the apartment.

see

PRACTICE 3: Word Order in Sentences

Put the words in the right order to make a sentence.

1. look at Kitty those anyway places to went

   Kitty _went to look at those places anyway._____.

2. dinner ask Let's to them soon

   Let's _____.

3. help find can you for apartments rent Ads

   Ads _____.

4. short to answers questions Write the

   Write _____.

5. did Jane share Kitty and costs What

   What _____?

6. did Kitty own her want Why apartment

   Why _____?

PRACTICE 4: Tag Questions

Write a question to finish the sentence.

1. You're glad you went to the reunion, _aren't you_____?

2. She is choking, _____?

3. There isn't a swimming pool, _____?

4. Parents want to keep you at home forever, _____?

5. Kitty O'Toole has made up her mind, _____?

6. This apartment is just right, _____?

7. Hugh was glad he went to the reunion, _____?

8. Computers help us in many ways, _____?

9. You have a Social Security card, _____?

10. Your Aunt Ellen will never eat barbecued ribs again, _____?

PRACTICE 5: Prepositions with Verbs

Write *to, for, with, up, in*

1. Kitty was living ___with___ her parents.

2. I have made _____ my mind.

3. She makes enough money to pay _____ food and rent.

4. I'm going to look _____ an apartment.

5. Sometimes I stay _____ late at night watching TV.

6. Kitty spoke _____ people at work and at church.

7. They shopped _____ a used sofa, a table, and some chairs.

8. Aunt Ellen argued _____ my father.

9. He had to sign _____ for classes.

10. My niece was playing _____ her friends.

11. My mother said _____ me, "I had a lot of fun."

12. Fill _____ the forms.

13. Pick _____ the books that are on the floor.

14. We listened _____ the stories.

15. You fill _____ boxes on the computer forms.

PRACTICE 6: *other, others,* and *another*

Write *another, other,* or *others* in each sentence.

1. He rescued his niece from the lake. The ___*others*___ were glad he rescued her.

2. I can afford this apartment. I can't afford the _____ one.

3. Then he told _____ family story.

4. We had a happy family reunion. I hope we have _____ one next year.

5. Some computer games can amuse you at home. _____ computer games are in shopping centers.

6. Some computers do just one job. _____ do many jobs.

7. I have a good black dress. I want _____ one.

8. Write on every _____ line.

9. Do you want _____ piece of ham?

10. My brother and his wife have one little girl. They want _____.

11. I have two nephews. One is seventeen. The _____ is fifteen.

12. A big wave hit my niece. Then _____ wave carried her into water over her head.

PRACTICE 7: Listen

Listen to the teacher. Write the word that is missing.

1. What do _____ want?

2. I want _____ eat at Fran's.

3. What do _____ want to eat?

4. I want _____ sandwich.

5. What do _____ want to drink?

6. I want a glass _____ milk.

Note to the teacher: Do not pronounce the missing words carefully or in an
exaggerated fashion. Say the sentences with natural speed
and intonation. Use the words in the answer key.

between (be tween')	mail	postal	(pōst' ul)
change (chānj)	*new	postage	(pōst' ij)

PRACTICE 8: Change of Address Form

Kitty O'Toole is moving from her parents' home at 12 Garden Street, Center City, New York 13202. She is going to live at 105 Parkview Street, Center City, New York 13207. She will live in apartment number 307 (No. 307). Kitty is moving on April 30, 1987.

Kitty wants the U.S. Postal Service (USPS) to send her mail to her new address, not the old one.

Fill in the Change of Address Form for Kitty. It will tell the U.S. Postal Service to bring her mail to her new apartment.

USPS CHANGE OF ADDRESS ORDER   **Please Print**

1. Change of address is for (check one):   [ ] Family   [ ] One person
2. I will pay postage on my fourth-class mail: [ ] Yes   [ ] No
3. Print last name:

4. Print first name of each person covered by this order.
   Leave a blank space between names.

5. Old Address   Number and street: Apt. No.

_____   _____

   City: State: Zip Code:

_____   _____ |__|__|__|__|__|

6. New Address   Number and street: Apt. No.

_____   _____

   City: State: Zip Code:

_____   _____ |__|__|__|__|__|

7. Show Date of Move: Month Day Year   8. Date Signed: Month Day Year

                     |__|__|__|__| |__|__|__|__|

9. Sign here (Do not print):

_____

PRACTICE 1: Write Sentences

Write 3 sentences. Tell what the flag of Canada looks like.

PRACTICE 2: Write Sentences

Write 3 sentences. Tell what the flag of the United States looks like.

PRACTICE 3: Make Negative Sentences

Write the sentence with *not*.

1. Fly the flag in the rain.

   Don't fly the flag in the rain.

2. Let the flag touch the floor.

   _____

3. The apartment was in a safe part of the city.

   _____

4. Let's quit for today.

   _____

5. Let's ask them to dinner.

   _____

6. Flag Day in the United States is on June 15.

   _____

7. The stars on the U.S. flag are red.

   _____

PRACTICE 4: Make Negative Sentences

Make the verb with *to* negative.

1. It's OK to arrive at the picnic on time.

   It's OK not to arrive at the picnic on time.

2. It's OK to ask Ann in the morning.

   _____

3. It's great to get up early in the morning.

   _____

4. It's rude to salute.

   _____

5. It's rude for a man to remove his hat.

   _____

PRACTICE 5: Word Order in Sentences

Add the words to the sentences.

1. (13, first) The stripes stand for the states.

   The stripes stand for the first 13 states.

2. (left, top) The corner of the flag is blue.

   _____

3. (red, maple) The leaf stands for the country of Canada.

   _____

4. (country's, his) It's rude for a man not to remove his hat for (the*) flag.

   _____

5. (safe, clean, 22) There were apartments in the building.

   _____

6. (clean, eat-in, large) There was a kitchen in the apartment.

   _____

PRACTICE 6: Write Sentences

Write sentences using *too* + adjective + *to* + verb.

1. too young to _My parents said I was too young to be on my own._

2. too old to _____

   _____

3. too big to _____

   _____

4. too far to _____

   _____

5. too windy to _____

   _____

* Do not use *the* when you add *country's* and *his*.

PRACTICE 7: Story with Missing Words

Write the missing words.

The Flag

People show their love for their country when they honor their flag. The bright colors of the flag _____ for the country, its people, and _____ ideas.

The flag of the United States _____ red, white, and blue. Red stands _____ courage. White stands for honor. And _____ stands for justice. The flag has 13 _____ of red and white. These stripes _____ for the first 13 states. The _____ left corner of the flag is _____ with 50 white stars. The stars _____ for the 50 states in the _____ States today. We sometimes give the U.S. _____ a name. One name we use _____ the Stars and Stripes.

Some people _____ that a leader of the country _____ the first U.S. flag. That may _____ true. Other people say that a _____ made the first flag in her _____. That may be true. We may _____ know the true story.

In the _____ States, people honor their flag on _____ 14. June 14 is Flag Day. _____ June 14, people fly the flag _____ their homes, businesses, and city buildings.

_____ flag of Canada is white with _____ red maple leaf on it. On _____ side of the maple leaf is _____ red stripe. The red maple leaf stands for the country of Canada.

PRACTICE 1: Prepositions

Write *at, by, for, from, on, up.*

1. Lewis came _from_ a poor family.

2. He grew _____ with very little money.

3. Lewis worked _____ the city on the sewers.

4. The crew laughed _____ him.

5. Judy looked _____ ways to save money.

6. Children, please pick _____ your clothes.

7. The Burns family was getting _____.

   They had enough money to live _____.

8. After he yelled _____ his son, he felt bad.

9. Lewis worked _____ the public works department.

10. Look _____ the number in the telephone directory.

11. Judy came _____ a family that wasn't rich.

12. Judy grew _____ with nice clothes and other things she wanted.

13. Judy stayed _____ home with the children.

14. Chew your meat or you will choke _____ it.

15. They sat on the steps and watched the traffic go _____.

ambulance	(am′ bū luns)	insurance	(in shur′ uns)
company	(cum′ pu ny)	library	(lī′ brār y)
hospital	(hos′ pit ul)		

PRACTICE 2: Telephone Numbers

Write the telephone numbers for your city.

Fire _____

Police _____

Doctor _____

Ambulance _____

Hospital _____

Car Insurance _____

Car Repair _____

Utility Company _____

Public Works (trash pickup) _____

Work _____

School _____

Library _____

Home _____

Relative _____

Telephone Information _____ + 555-1212
            (Area Code)

Note to the teacher: Help the student find any numbers he does not know.

For pronunciation, help the student with the pronunciation of any numbers he has difficulty with. Teach the pauses (555-12-12) as well.

PRACTICE 3: *a, an, the*

Write *a, an, the,* or, if no word is needed, an X.

A. ___X___ Lewis worked for __the__ city on __the__ sewers. He was on _____ work crew. _____ crew of workers cleaned _____ sewers. _____ dirt and leaves got into _____ sewers. _____ work crew used _____ machines to remove _____ dirt and leaves. _____ machine threw _____ dirt and leaves into _____ truck.

B. _____ Kitty wanted _____ apartment of her own. She looked at _____ ads for _____ apartments in _____ Sunday paper. She hoped to find _____ apartment in _____ building with _____ pool. _____ places she was able to afford were not in _____ safe part of _____ city.

C. This is _____ age of _____ computer. _____ computer is _____ machine that works with _____ facts like _____ names and addresses. It works with _____ facts like _____ prices and _____ lists of things in _____ stores.

Some computers do just one job. Some do many jobs. _____ computer that does many jobs may be huge or little. It may be so huge that it fills _____ big office. Or _____ computer may be as little as _____ table radio.

PRACTICE 4: Combine Sentences

Combine the sentences. Use *until*.

1. We won't get married. We have enough money.

   We won't get married until we have enough money.

2. Judy worked. Her baby was born. _____

3. She worked. She became tired. _____

4. Write. I tell you to stop. _____

5. Sit here. Someone calls your name.

   _____

6. She was in the water. I rescued her.

   _____

7. He didn't say anything. Dinner was over.

   _____

8. They worked on the sewers. They were clean.

   _____

9. We will stay. The fireworks are over.

   _____

10. Judy stayed home with the children. They went to school.

    _____

    _____

11. Kitty looked for apartments. She got tired.

    _____

    _____

12. We are going to sit in the car. It's time to go in the house.

    _____

    _____

PRACTICE 5: Story with Missing Words

Write the missing words.

The Family Jewels

Lewis Burns came from a poor family. He grew up with very little

_____. As a child, Lewis said to _____, "When I grow up, I will

_____ be poor. When I grow up, _____ will have a fine car. My

_____ will wear jewels. We will have _____ fine home."

Lewis had this dream _____ he grew up. He went to _____

until his father died. Then Lewis _____ to grow up in a hurry.

_____ quit school and went to work.

_____ worked for the city on the _____. He was on a work

crew. _____ crew of workers cleaned the sewers. _____ and leaves

got into the sewers. _____ work crew used a machine to _____

the dirt and leaves. The machine _____ the dirt and leaves into a

_____.

It was a dirty job. But _____ went to work every day in _____

clothes. The crew laughed at him. "_____ at Lewis," they said. "He

looks _____ a cool cat in the morning. _____ by evening he

looks like a _____ rat."

When Lewis was 20, he _____ Judy. Judy's family wasn't rich. But

_____ had more money than Lewis's family. _____ grew up with

nice clothes and _____ things she wanted.

PRACTICE 1: Pronouns

Write *myself, himself, herself,* or *yourself.*

1. "Another *F* in math!" he said to _*himself*_.

2. You must help _____.

3. The girl said something to _____.

4. I believe in _____, too.

5. You did most of it _____.

6. "I love Judy," Lewis said to _____.

PRACTICE 2: Word Order in Sentences

Add the word to the sentences.

1. (very) He felt blue.

   He felt very blue. _____

2. (enough) He did well in his other classes.

   _____

3. (church) Duke knew Mr. Newman from camp.

   _____

4. (next) I'll be 16 Tuesday.

   _____

5. (just) Duke needed some help.

   _____

6. (too) Duke started doing his math lessons at school.

   _____

7. (yourself) You did most of it.

   _____

8. (never) Mr. Newman made Duke feel stupid.

   _____

PRACTICE 3: Combine Sentences

Combine the two sentences into one.

1. He got his report card. He felt very blue.

   When he got his report card, he felt very blue.

2. Duke asked to speak to Jack Newman. He ran the press room.

3. Jack believed. Duke needed some help.

4. They give services to people. People live in the city.

5. I will not be poor. I grow up.

6. He loves me. I love him.

7. I will have a fine car. I grow up.

8. Sometimes I stay up late. I play my radio quietly.

9. Lewis was 20. He met Judy.

10. They had enough money to live on. They didn't own their own home.

11. A computer is a machine. The computer works with facts like names and addresses.

PRACTICE 4: Write Sentences

Write sentences using an adjective + *enough* + *to* + verb.

1. old enough to _Duke wasn't old enough to quit school._ _____

_____

2. big enough to _____

_____

3. heavy enough to _____

_____

4. bright enough to _____

_____

5. fast enough to _____

_____

6. interested enough to _____

_____

PRACTICE 5: Write Sentences

Write sentences. Tell about a thing you had better do.

1. _I had better clean my apartment._ _____

2. _____

_____

3. _____

_____

4. _____

_____

5. _____

_____

6. _____

_____

PRACTICE 6: Story with Missing Words

Write the missing words.

A New Start

Duke Miller was a student at Lake Avenue High School. When he got his

report _____ on Tuesday, he felt very _____. "Another *F* in

math!" he _____ to himself. "It's no use! _____ will never pass

this stupid _____! I'm going to quit school _____ get a job!"

Duke needed _____ to finish high school. He _____ well

enough in his other _____. But math didn't interest him. _____

didn't understand it. And that _____ him feel stupid.

After school _____ day, Duke went to the _____ of the *Oak

Park News.* _____ hoped to find a job _____ the press room.

That was _____ the newspaper was printed. Duke _____ to speak

to Jack Newman, _____ ran the press room. Duke _____ Mr.

Newman from church camp. _____ Newman was the sports coach

_____.

Duke told Mr. Newman that _____ was looking for a job. "_____

you're still a student, aren't _____?" asked Mr. Newman.

"Yes, I'm _____ student. But I'm thinking of _____ school,"

Duke answered. "I'll be 16 _____ Tuesday. I'll be old enough _____

quit then."

"What's the matter _____ school?" asked Mr. Newman.

"It's _____ stupid math class!" Duke said. "_____ can't pass

it no matter _____ I do. But I don't need math to run a printing

press, do I?"

PRACTICE 1: Verb Forms

Write *is* or *are*.

1. Here __are__ some ideas for reading your daily newspaper.

2. You can see where each of the Five *W*'s _____.

3. There _____ no cure for the kind of cancer the boy has.

4. The main news _____ on the first page of the paper.

5. The utility company _____ asking to raise its rates.

6. The headlines _____ in large print.

7. Here _____ the book you want.

8. There _____ the books I want to read.

PRACTICE 2: *to* and *too*

Write *to* or *too*.

1. We need __to__ think of the future.

2. The Lions Club agreed _____ raise $1,000.

3. The zoo is _____ cool for the animals in winter.

4. The hearings will be open _____ the public.

5. _____ many lions have to live together.

6. There were _____ many people in the car.

7. They agreed _____ raise money for the zoo.

8. You shouldn't give him _____ much help.

PRACTICE 3: Make Questions

Write questions with *who, what, where,* or *when.*
Ask about the underlined words.

1. Dr. Luther thanked <u>the tutors</u> for their service.

   Who did Dr. Luther thank for their service?

2. Mrs. Hoover told the police <u>that a gold ring was missing</u>.

   _____

3. The fire department rescued Mike O'Toole from <u>the Union Building</u>.

   _____

4. O'Toole will begin his climb <u>at 7 a.m.</u>

   _____

5. The Lions Club agreed <u>to raise $1,000 to keep the lions in the zoo</u>.

   _____

6. Tutors can get application forms <u>from the school board office</u>.

   _____

7. Mike Romano spoke for <u>a group of business leaders</u>.

   _____

8. She thanked the tutors for <u>their service</u>.

   _____

9. Lewis died <u>last year</u>.

   _____

10. The fire fighters carried the rope <u>up to the thirty-fourth floor</u>.

    _____

PRACTICE 4: Combine Sentences

Combine the two sentences into one.

1. At the hearing, Arthur Newman spoke first.
   He is the president of the utility company.

   At the hearing, Arthur Newman, the president of the utility company, spoke first.

2. The young singer left his three sports cars to his cousin, Luke Jones.
   He led Lewis's band.

   _____

   _____

3. "This city needs a better zoo," said Hugh Baker.
   He is the public information officer for the Huron City Zoo.

   _____

   _____

4. Lewis left his shares to his aunt, Judy Jones.
   She raised him after his parents died.

   _____

   _____

5. O'Toole was trying to climb the side of the Union Building.
   He says he is a human fly.

   _____

   _____

6. Dr. Mary Luther was the main speaker of the evening.
   She is president of the school board.

   _____

   _____

PRACTICE 5: Word Order in Sentences

Put the words in the right order to make a sentence.

1. news five tells story Each things

   Each news story tells five things.

2. public The will hearings open be to the

   _____

3. died Lewis 27 the at last age of year

   _____

4. left Lewis his in grandmother home Florida his and grandfather to

   _____

   _____

5. 5,000 Every go people week the to zoo

   _____

6. math You or have reading each a helped student in

   _____

   _____

7. Mrs. and apartment Mr. Hoover's into afternoon was yesterday broken

   _____

   _____

8. The tell that children the me a like lot zoo they

   _____

   _____

PRACTICE 6: Combine Sentences

Combine the two sentences into one. Use *so . . . that.*

1. There are many people at the zoo. It's hard to see the animals.

   There are so many people at the zoo that it's hard to see the animals.

2. People were amused. They laughed at Mike O'Toole.

   _____

   _____

3. His music was good. It won him four gold records.

   _____

   _____

4. Many people spoke at the hearings. They had to be continued on another day.

   _____

   _____

5. Duke felt blue about getting an *F* in math. He wanted to quit school.

   _____

   _____

PRACTICE 7: Listen

Circle the letter of the sentence the teacher says.

1. a. He will move to a bigger apartment.

   b. He'll move to a bigger apartment.

2. a. We are happy that you are here.

   b. We're happy that you are here.

3. a. I have lived in Central City for three years.

   b. I've lived in Central City for three years.

4. a. Who is in the kitchen?

   b. Who's in the kitchen?

5. a. She is going to help me.

   b. She's going to help me.

Note to the teacher: In each item, read *a* or *b*. Do not choose the same letter
each time.

PRACTICE 1: *no, not*

Write *no* or *not*.

1. He has __*no*__ way of passing on what he knows to others.

2. Jake didn't care if people understood him or _____.

3. He has _____ relatives.

4. "It's _____ too far," Jake said.

5. Jake Bush has _____ money.

6. Jake knew which plants were good to eat and which ones were _____ safe.

PRACTICE 2: *wh-* Words

Write *what, where, when, why,* or *which.*

1. Someone wrote a book to share __*what*__ that man knew.

2. No one knew _____ Jake wanted to live alone in the woods.

3. Jake knew _____ plants were good to eat and _____ ones were not safe.

4. I didn't think you understood _____ I love the woods.

5. You can find the page on _____ each chapter begins.

6. New businesses will not come here _____ they can get cheaper rates in other cities.

7. O'Toole was near the thirty-third floor _____ he got stuck.

8. He had been stuck for 20 minutes _____ the fire department came to the rescue.

9. The press room was _____ the paper was printed.

10. I can't pass math no matter _____ I do.

11. Read the telephone listing for some of the city offices _____ Lewis lived.

12. A security deposit is money you pay _____ you move in.

PRACTICE 3: Sentence Order

Put the sentences in the right order to make a story. First, number them in the right order.

_____ Jake Bush lived alone in the woods.

_____ And that way was 15 miles each way on foot.

_____ Jake went to the store only a few times a year.

_____ There was only one way from Jake's home in the hills to the store.

_____ He went there to buy coffee, sugar, fish hooks, and a few other things.

Now write the sentences. (Do not write the numbers.)

Jake Bush _____

_____

_____

_____

_____

_____

_____

_____

_____

Note to the teacher: Have the student read the sentences aloud in his numbered
order before he writes them out. This will help him determine
if his order is correct.

PRACTICE 4: Word Order in Sentences

Add *hardly ever* to the sentences.

1. Jake said something.

   Jake hardly ever said anything.

2. He was sick.

   _____

3. Jake went to the store.

   _____

4. Duke is late.

   _____

5. He speaks to someone.

   _____

6. Jake asks someone for help.

   _____

7. Ann is sad.

   _____

PRACTICE 5: Tag Questions

Write a question to finish the sentence.

1. Duke is hardly ever late, __*is he*__?

2. Hugh's family hardly ever gets together, _____?

3. Jake was hardly ever sick, _____?

4. Jake hardly ever went to the store, _____?

5. Kitty and her roommate hardly ever stay home from work, _____?

6. Ann is hardly ever sad, _____?

7. Sam hardly ever speaks to Jim, _____?

8. She hardly ever baked a cake for him, _____?

Note to the teacher: Remind the student that a sentence with *hardly ever* is considered negative. Tag questions will be in the affirmative.

PRACTICE 6: *can* and *could*

Add *can* or *could* to the sentences.

1. He never tried to catch more fish than he _could_ eat.

   He never tries to catch more fish than he _can_ eat.

2. He knows that Hugh _____ swim.

   He knew that Hugh _____ swim.

3. I am sure that I _____ live by myself.

   I was sure that I _____ live by myself.

4. I hope that I _____ find a roommate.

   I hoped that I _____ find a roommate.

5. Jane says she _____ swim.

   Jane said she _____ swim.

PRACTICE 7: Write Sentences

Write sentences. Tell what you would like to do.

1. _I would like to speak English well._

2. _____

   _____

3. _____

   _____

4. _____

   _____

5. _____

   _____

6. _____

   _____

PRACTICE 8: Story with Missing Words

Write the missing words.

The Good Life in the Woods

No one understood Jake Bush. No one understood why he _____ to live alone in the _____. At 83, Jake Bush was _____ alone in the north woods _____ New York State. He had _____ there for 30 years.

Jake _____ care if people understood him _____ not. To him, life in _____ woods was good.

Jake Bush _____ in a one-room cabin _____ a beautiful brook. The brook _____ full of fish. Jake could _____ fish every time he threw _____ hook into the water. He _____ fish home to cook every _____. He took his drinking water _____ the brook, too.

The woods _____ full of wild plants. Jake _____ many kinds of these plants _____ food. He knew which plants _____ good to eat and which _____ were not safe.

Jake cooked _____ heated his cabin with a wood-burning _____. He cut wood for his _____ from dead trees. He cut _____ the big trees. Then he _____ and pulled the heavy pieces _____ to his cabin. He cut _____ into little pieces for his _____.

PRACTICE 1: Prepositions with Verbs

Write *over, out of, up, on, out.*

1. Many people moved _out of_ the south side.

2. They worked _____ one problem at a time.

3. Some owners stopped paying taxes, and the city took _____ their houses.

4. The city council said that it would board _____ the houses.

5. "Don't board them _____! Fix them _____ instead!" one man shouted.

6. The council found _____ that the state had thousands of dollars for housing loans.

7. Some people cleaned _____ trash and broken glass around the park.

8. This book will pass _____ to others many of the things you know.

9. Jake will never move _____ the woods.

PRACTICE 2: *since* and *for*

Write *since* or *for.*

1. The houses had been standing _since_ about 1900.

2. Some older people had owned their homes _____ many years.

3. Duke has been studying _____ after dinner.

4. Jake Bush lived in the woods _____ 30 years.

5. I have lived in my house _____ six years.

6. Judy and Lewis have been married _____ 1980.

7. Lewis has worked for the public works department _____ he quit school.

8. Mr. Newman helped Duke with his math _____ six months.

candy	(can' dy)	restroom	(rest' room)	sweet	
outlet	(out' let)	shoe	(shoo)	video	(vid' ē ō)

PRACTICE 3: Read a Map

This is a map of the Mountain City Shopping Center. Study the map before answering the questions.

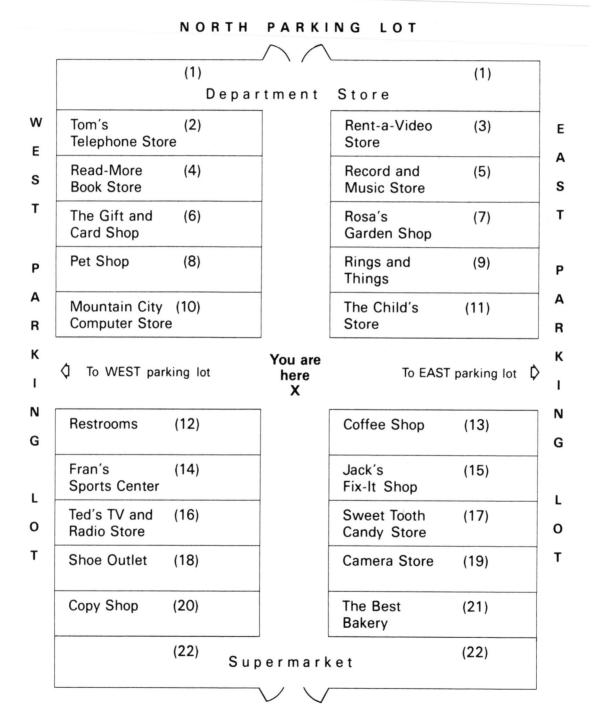

A. Give short answers to the questions. Use the map to find the answers.

1. Where is the Best Bakery? *21 (next to the Camera Store)*

2. Where are the restrooms? _____

3. Where can you buy a dog? _____

4. Where can you buy earrings? _____

5. Where can you get a sandwich? _____

6. Where can you buy running shoes? _____

7. Where can you get a key made? _____

8. Where can you buy a cook book? _____

9. Where is the Copy Shop? _____

10. Where is the Child's Store? _____

B. You are going to the Mountain City Shopping Center to do some shopping. You are going to look at a computer. You are going to buy a book about computers, a child's game, a birthday card and a ball. While you are there, you will have a snack.

Write about your shopping plans. Where will you park? What will you do first, second, and after that?

_____

_____

_____

_____

_____

_____

_____

_____

_____

_____

PRACTICE 4: Word Order in Sentences

Put the words in the right order to make a sentence.

1. up them Don't board !

   <u>Don't board them up!</u>

2. houses said of had they money owners no Many

   _____

3. South went large a to city council Side group Neighbors of meeting A

   _____

4. instead up them Fix !

   _____

5. are to afraid old out people Our go !

   _____

6. streets They and were of parks proud clean their

   _____

PRACTICE 5: Pronouns

Circle the right word in each sentence.

1. They formed a group to do (anything, (something)) about their problems.
2. They discussed their problems with (anyone, someone) on the city council.
3. (Someone, Anyone) pushed her to the ground.
4. They could not do (anything, something) without money.
5. (Some, Any) people formed a Neighborhood Watch.
6. I could learn (some, any) things from watching you.
7. They couldn't do (something, anything) about the houses.

PRACTICE 6: Write Sentences

Write sentences using *It's not safe to*.

1. *It's not safe to go by an empty house on foot.*

2.

3.

4.

5.

PRACTICE 7: Write Sentences

Write sentences using *proud of*.

1. *The South Side Neighbors are proud of their clean parks.*

2.

3.

4.

5.

PRACTICE 8: Write Sentences

Write sentences using *take turns* + verb-*ing*.

1. *My husband and I take turns doing the dishes.*
2. _____
3. _____
4. _____
   _____
5. _____
   _____

PRACTICE 9: Listen

Circle the letter of the sentence that the teacher says.

1. a. What is it?

   b. Where is it?

2. a. Where is he going?

   b. When is he going?

3. a. What's the book?

   b. Where's the book?

4. a. When's the party?

   b. Where's the party?

Note to the teacher: In each item, read *a* or *b*. Do not choose the same letter each
time. Use contractions. Pronounce the sentence with natural
speed and intonation.

schedule   (skej′ule)

PRACTICE 1: Read a Schedule

Read the Howard County Fair schedule for Friday.

Howard County Fair Schedule: Friday	
8:00 a.m.	Howard County Fair opens
9:00 a.m.	Flower Show
10:00 a.m.	Pie Contest
1:00 p.m.	Tractor-Pulling Contest
4:30 p.m.	Horse Races
5:30 p.m.	Best Animal Contest
7:00 p.m.	Rock Concert
9:30 p.m.	Fireworks

PRACTICE 2: Write a Letter

Write a letter to your friend. Tell your friend about the Howard County Fair.
Tell what you are going to do at the fair. Use the schedule.

Dear _____,

    I am going to the Howard County Fair. _____

_____

_____

_____

_____

_____

_____

_____

_____

                    Your friend,

                    _____

                    (Sign your name.)

PRACTICE 3: *how* + *to* + Verb

Combine the two sentences. Use *how to*.

1. I know. I can drive a tractor.

    I know how to drive a tractor.

2. Mrs. Brown knows. She can bake an apple pie.

    _____

3. The clowns know. They make the crowd laugh.

    _____

4. Jake knew. He cured himself.

    _____

5. Sam learned. He lived in the woods.

    _____

6. The tutors know. They help students in reading and math.

    _____

7. She learned. She can speak in public.

    _____

PRACTICE 4: Write Sentences

Write sentences. Tell what you know how to do. Use *how to* in each sentence.

1. *I know how to report a fire.*
2. _____
3. _____
4. _____
5. _____
6. _____
7. _____
8. _____

PRACTICE 5: Combine Sentences

Combine the two sentences using *how* plus the word that is underlined.

1. The riders showed. Their horses followed orders very <u>well</u>.

   The riders showed how well their horses followed orders.

2. He is telling us. Old people are <u>afraid</u> to go out.

   He is telling us how afraid old people are to go out.

3. He learned. It was <u>easy</u> to ride a horse.

4. We know. The clowns make the crowd <u>happy</u>.

5. Sue and Tom know. The rides are <u>exciting</u>.

6. We can tell. Sue is <u>proud</u> of her horse.

7. He knows. It's <u>far</u> from here to Sugar Hill.

8. We watched. It was <u>hard</u> for the tractor to pull against the machine.

9. Tom showed. He was <u>unhappy</u> not to win first prize.

10. No one knows. Duke is <u>interested</u> in sports.

$$\boxed{\text{lottery} \quad (\text{lot' er y})}$$

PRACTICE 6: Read and Write Numbers

Read the story and write the numbers.

The State Lottery

Lewis won money in the state lottery. He was the winner with five other people. The prize was $2,490,000. Each winner won $415,000. Each winner will get $20,750 each year for twenty years.

A. Write the numbers for these words.

two million four hundred ninety thousand _____

four hundred fifteen thousand _____

twenty thousand seven hundred fifty _____

fifteen thousand two hundred _____

sixty million two hundred thousand _____

B. Write the words for these numbers.

690,000 _____

5,000 _____

300,500 _____

1,000,000 _____

100,000 _____

23,600 _____

722 _____

PRACTICE 7: Rejoinders

Read the sentence. Then write an answer using *That's easy for you to say* and another sentence.

1. Jane (from the United States) said, "English isn't hard."

   That's easy for you to say. You grew up in the United States.

2. Mrs. Black (a math teacher) said, "Math is not hard."

   _____

   _____

3. Mr. Brown (a bus driver) said, "Driving a bus is not hard."

   _____

   _____

4. Kitty (from the United States) said, "Reading books in English is easy."

   _____

   _____

5. Hugh (a swimmer) said, "Rescuing someone from the water is not hard."

   _____

   _____

6. Sue (a horse rider) said, "Winning a horse show is fun. It's not hard."

   _____

   _____

PRACTICE 8: Story with Missing Words

Write the missing words.

At the Howard County Fair

Mr. and Mrs. Ed Brown and their two teenagers were in town for the county fair. The Howard County Fair was held _____ Johnstown at the end of the _____. Every summer, crowds of people came _____ town for the fair. The week _____ the fair was the most exciting _____ of the year in Johnstown.

The _____ lived on a farm in Howard _____. They had worked hard to get _____ for the fair.

The Browns' son _____ hoped to win a blue ribbon _____ his cow Beauty. He had raised _____ cow from birth. Beauty gave more _____ than any other cow on their _____. Tom was sure that she would _____ first prize.

Tom's sister Sue was _____ about the horse show. Last year, _____ and her horse Sugar won a _____ ribbon for second prize. "I'm sure _____ Sugar is ready for a blue _____ now," Sue told her brother.

Tom _____ , "Yes, and Beauty is ready now, _____."

At the fair, Sue found a _____ for Sugar in the horse barn. _____ Tom put Beauty in the cow _____.

Mrs. Brown took her flowers to _____ flower show. It was held in _____ morning. There were many kinds of _____ in the show. Mary Brown got _____ blue ribbon for her yellow roses. _____ the apple pie she took to _____ pie contest didn't win any prize.

PRACTICE 1: Polite Requests

Use *would* to make a request.

1. Ask Jake to teach you about the woods.

   Would you teach me about the woods ?

2. Ask Jake to let you watch him carve something.

   _____

3. Ask the city to let you borrow money for home repairs.

   _____

4. Ask Sue and Tom to watch the fireworks with you.

   _____

5. Ask Gladys to run for the city council.

   _____

6. Ask Sam to tell the story to the newspapers.

   _____

PRACTICE 2: Write Sentences

Write sentences using *would* to make a request.

1. *Would you like to have a cup of coffee with me?*

2. _____

   _____

3. _____

   _____

4. _____

   _____

5. _____

   _____

PRACTICE 3: Polite Replies

Read the polite replies. Can you think of more of them?

Sure.
Yes, I'd be happy to.
Yes, thank you.

No, thank you.
I'm sorry but I can't.
I'm sorry but I don't have time.

Give two answers to each of the questions.
Use the replies above or give one of your own.

1. Would you like a piece of pie?

    a. _Yes, thank you._   b. _No, I can't eat pie._

2. Would you help me move this log?

    a. _____   b. _____

3. Would you like to go to the Fair?

    a. _____   b. _____

4. Would you vote for Gladys Brooks?

    a. _____   b. _____

5. Would you like to visit the Brown farm?

    a. _____   b. _____

Note to the teacher: Students may give either negative or affirmative answers
                     to the questions.

PRACTICE 4: Verb Tenses

Write the correct form of the verb in the sentence.

When Sam Cook's book came out, the state (find) *found* out
that Jake Bush (live) _____ on state land.

Officers of the state parks department (discuss) _____ what to
do about Jake. "People (not be allowed) _____ to live on state
land," they said. "Mr. Bush (have) _____ to move."

An officer told Jake what the parks department (say) _____.

Jake (frown) _____ and (say) _____ "I (live)
_____ here for 30 years. Why are you (tell) _____ me
this now?"

The officer (answer) _____, "A lot of people (know)
_____ about you now. If we allow you to stay here, everyone (want)
_____ to live on free land."

Jake (get) _____ angry. "I'm not (move) _____!" he
shouted. "If you want me out, you (have) _____ to carry me out!"

PRACTICE 5: no, not

Write *no* or *not* in the sentence.

1. There was __*no*__ electric power.

2. Jake said, "I'm _____ moving."

3. They had _____ electric lights.

4. People are _____ allowed to live on state land.

5. They had _____ telephones.

6. It's _____ safe for children to play with matches.

PRACTICE 6: *a, an, the*

Write *a*, *an*, or *the*.

1. Gladys Brooks lived on ___the___ south side of Mountain City.

2. Gladys worked with _____ South Side Neighbors.

3. When _____ people of Mountain City voted, Gladys Brooks won _____ place on _____ city council.

4. _____ Browns got _____ telephone and _____ radio sometime in _____ 1920s.

5. They got _____ old car. With _____ car, they could go into Johnston quickly.

6. There is _____ apple in the box.

7. Mrs. Brown won _____ blue ribbon at _____ flower show.

8. Tom was _____ only one in his family who didn't win _____ blue ribbon.

9. _____ old man shouted, "Our old people are afraid to go out!"

10. At _____ hearing, Arthur Newman, president of _____ utility company, spoke first.

    He said, "_____ costs of running _____ utility company are going up."

11. _____ maple tree on this street has pretty leaves.

12. _____ Brown farm is like many family farms in America. Over _____ years, many changes have come to America's farms.

PRACTICE 7: Write Sentences

You have a friend who is late for work, smokes a lot, and eats too much. Your friend spends too much money. Tell your friend what to do to make her or his life better. Use *should* or *should not*.

1. *You should get to work on time.*

2. _____

3. _____

4. _____

5. _____

6. _____

7. _____

8. _____

PRACTICE 8: Listen

Listen to the teacher. Write the words (verbs) that are missing.

Jake Bush _____ on White Mountain in a state park. He _____ to stay in
                        (1)   (2)

his home. But officers of the state park _____ he _____ to leave. Jake
                                                              (3)   (4)

_____ angry with the officers. He shouted, "If you _____ me to move, you
        (5)   (6)

_____ have to carry me out. I _____ right here."
        (7)   (8)

Note to the teacher: Read the paragraph with normal speed and intonation. Do
                    not pronounce too carefully. Use the verbs in the answer key.

Lesson 12

PRACTICE 1: Adjectives and Other Modifiers

Put the words in the right order in the sentence.

1. (strong, big) The Shaws had a dog.

   The Shaws had a big, strong dog.

2. (empty, big) The fire started in a house.

   _____

3. (awful) Your dog has made a hole in my lawn.

   _____

4. (big, light gray) It was a(n) automobile.

   _____

5. (first, my, bad) I had (an) accident on Main Street.

   _____

6. (black, best) My dress is being repaired.

   _____

7. (new, fine) We will have a house.

   _____

8. (cotton, yellow, new) My dress is in the bedroom closet.

   _____

9. (gold, four) His music won him records.

   _____

10. (1983, Ford, brown) Your car was hit by a car.

   _____

   _____

Note to the teacher: Be sure students understand that words or letters in the
sentences that are within parentheses ( ) may not be needed
when the other words are added.

PRACTICE 2: Combine Sentences

Make one sentence from two. Use *to* + a verb.

1. It was hard. I couldn't see the exit sign in the fog.

   It was hard to see the exit sign in the fog.

2. It is not safe. We can't go by an empty house on foot.

   _____

   _____

3. It was hard. I couldn't drive on the snowy road.

   _____

   _____

4. It is good. I can see you again.

   _____

5. It's time. I will move into my own apartment.

   _____

   _____

6. It's rude. You shouldn't talk with food in your mouth.

   _____

   _____

7. It's time. The city will get a better zoo.

   _____

8. My mother was glad. She saw her nieces.

   _____

9. These plants are good. You can eat them.

   _____

10. We are afraid. We can't go out alone.

   _____

PRACTICE 3: Answer Questions

Write answers to these questions that people use many times.

1. What happened?

   I had an accident.

2. How are you?

   _____

3. What happened to you?

   _____

4. What's the matter?

   _____

5. You need help. What can I do?

   _____

6. Would you like a cup of coffee?

   _____

PRACTICE 4: Answer Questions

Write answers to the questions. Use *because of* and the words that are given.

1. Why couldn't the truck stop? (the wet road)

   The truck couldn't stop because of the wet road.

2. Why couldn't Paul see? (the fog)

   _____

3. Why can't the dog run free? (the city law)

   _____

4. Why was Paul unhappy? (the car accident)

   _____

5. Why was Duke so blue? (his report card)

   _____

6. Why was Jerry Dawson angry? (Bob's dog)

   _____

PRACTICE 5: Answer Questions

Answer the questions. Use *hardly*.

1. Could Paul see the road?

Paul could hardly see the road because of the fog.

2. Could Paul stop his car in time?

_____

3. Did Jake say something in answer to Sam's questions?

_____

_____

4. Could Joe Brunoski speak some English at first?

_____

_____

5. Would Jerry Dawson speak to Bob Shaw?

_____

6. Does the city council agree on something?

_____

PRACTICE 6: Tag Questions

Write a question to finish the sentence.

1. Paul could hardly see the road, *could he* _____?

2. Paul could hardly stop his car in time, _____?

3. Jake said hardly anything to Sam, _____?

4. Joe Brunoski hardly spoke any English, _____?

5. Jerry would hardly speak to Bob, _____?

6. The city council hardly agrees on anything, _____?

Note to the teacher: Remind the student that a sentence with *hardly* is considered
negative. Tag questions after *hardly* will be in the affirmative.

PRACTICE 7: Story with Missing Words

Write the missing words.

The Neighbors' Dog

Jerry Dawson had a beautiful lawn. His neighbors, the Shaws, had a _____, strong dog. Their dog liked to _____ holes with his long claws.

One _____ morning, Jerry Dawson was cutting his _____. He saw a big hole in _____ lawn near the fence. Jerry Dawson _____ across the fence to Bob Shaw. "_____ dog has made an awful hole _____ my lawn again. He crawled under _____ fence. I can see his claw _____."

Bob Shaw came to the fence. _____ saw why Jerry Dawson was so _____. "I'm awfully sorry," Bob said. "But _____ can I do? He's a strong _____. He can dig a hole under _____ fence with his long claws."

"Being _____ isn't good enough," said Jerry. "Tie _____ up. That's the law. You know _____ law of this town as well _____ I do. It's against the law _____ let a dog run free."

"I _____ let my dog run free on _____ streets," said Bob. "The law says _____ dog doesn't have to be tied _____ if you have a fence around _____ land. I don't want to tie _____ dog up. I need him as _____ watchdog."

"I'm sorry, but this has _____ going on long enough," said Jerry. "_____ have to fix the fence so _____ dog can't crawl under it. He _____ better not dig any more holes _____ my lawn, or I'll report you _____ the police!" By that time, Bob _____ awfully angry, too. Both men were _____ across the fence.

Edward (Ed' werd)	Frances (Fran' ses)
Elizabeth (Ē liz' u beth)	Pamela (Pam' e lu)

PRACTICE 1: Names

Write sentences using *call* and the names in the list.

Fran	Bob	Jimmy
Kit	Dave	Luke
Liz	Ed	Tommy
Molly	Jack	
Pam		

1. His name is Edward.   We call him __*Ed.*_____

2. Her name is Kitty.   We call her _____

3. His name is Jim.   _____

4. His name is Robert.   _____

5. His name is Tom.   _____

6. His name is Luke.   _____

7. Her name is Frances.   _____

8. Her name is Elizabeth.   _____

9. His name is David.   _____

10. Her name is Pamela.   _____

11. His name is John.   _____

12. Her name is Molly.   _____

Note to the teacher: Be sure the student knows which names are used for males, which for females, and which for both (Fran and Kit, nicknames only).

PRACTICE 2: *will* and *would*

Use *will* or *would* in the sentences.

1. He thinks the fans ___*will*___ call him names.

   He thought the fans ___*would*___ call him names.

2. He says he _____ play baseball.

   He said he _____ play baseball.

3. He says he _____ take the dog for a walk.

   He said he _____ take the dog for a walk.

4. Kitty says she _____ swim.

   Kitty said she _____ swim.

5. I hope that I _____ find a roommate.

   I hoped that I _____ find a roommate.

PRACTICE 3: Answer Questions

Answer the questions. Use *It takes*.

1. How long does it take to go from your house to the park?

   It takes twenty minutes to go from my house to the park.

2. How long does it take to go from your house to the high school?

   _____

   _____

3. How long does it take to go from your house to church?

   _____

4. How long does it take to go from your city to New York City by car?

   _____

   _____

5. How long does it take to go from your house to work?

   _____

6. How long does it take to go from your house to the city zoo?

   _____

PRACTICE 4: Prepositions with Verbs

Write *out, up,* or *with* in the sentence.

1. Jerry Dawson was angry _with_ Bob Shaw.

2. Bob Shaw didn't want to tie _____ his dog.

3. You need to find _____ some information.

4. It takes a strong man to stand _____ to prejudice.

5. When he got _____ of the armed services, he played baseball.

6. The dog's barking woke Jerry _____.

7. Paul was covered _____ tomato sauce.

8. When Sam's book came _____, the state found _____ that Jake Bush was living on state land.

9. She worked _____ the South Side Neighbors on housing problems.

10. Each tractor was hooked _____ to the pulling contest machine.

PRACTICE 5: Listen

Circle the letter of the sentence the teacher says.

1. a. She could read when she was seven.

   b. She couldn't read when she was seven.

2. a. She can swim.

   b. She can't swim.

3. a. Could you help Ann?

   b. Couldn't you help Ann?

4. a. Can you speak English?

   b. Can't you speak English?

5. a. Ed can watch TV in the morning.

   b. Ed can't watch TV in the morning.

Note to the teacher: In each item, read either *a* or *b*. Do not choose the same letter each time. Read the sentences with natural speed and intonation.

PRACTICE 6: Sentence Order

Put the sentences in the right order to make a story. First, number them in the right order.

_____ In 1947, he started playing with the Brooklyn Dodgers baseball team.

_____ Jackie played with the Dodgers for 10 years.

_____ Jackie Robinson was born in the South in 1919.

_____ In 1962, he was voted into the Baseball Hall of Fame.

_____ In 1955, he led the Dodgers to win the World Series.

Now write the sentences. (Do not write the numbers.)

_____

_____

_____

_____

_____

_____

_____

_____

_____

_____

_____

_____

Note to the teacher: Have the student read the sentences aloud in his numbered order before he writes them out. This will help him determine if his order is correct.

PRACTICE 1: Make Negative Questions

Make a negative question from the sentence.

1. You want to marry again.

   Don't you want to marry again?

2. You forgot something.

   _____

3. Your family would like some fresh fish.

   _____

4. It feels good to sit down.

   _____

5. He's handsome!

   _____

6. Canada has Thanksgiving Day in October.

   _____

7. Jackie Robinson was the first black player in the major leagues.

   _____

   _____

8. You like to watch television.

   _____

9. Jake wants to stay in the woods forever.

   _____

10. This is the best book you have ever read.

    _____

PRACTICE 2: Verb Tenses

Use the right form of the verb in the sentence.

1. Kay (have) __*has*__ lunch with her friend every day.

   Kay (have) __*had*__ lunch with her friend yesterday.

   Kay (have) __*has had*__ lunch with her friend every day this week.

2. Lan (buy) _____ some new things for her class every month.

   Lan (buy) _____ some new pencils yesterday.

   Lan (buy) _____ many things for class since class started.

3. Lan (think) _____ about Viet Nam every day.

   Lan (think) _____ about Viet Nam yesterday.

   Lan (think) _____ about Viet Nam every day since she left.

4. Molly (bring) _____ her lunch to work every day.

   Molly (bring) _____ her lunch to work yesterday.

   Molly (bring) _____ her lunch every day since she started to work.

5. Tom (catch) _____ cold easily.

   Tom (catch) _____ a cold last week.

   Tom (catch) _____ many colds since he moved to New York.

6. Jerry and Bob always (fight) _____ about Bob's dog.

   Jerry and Bob (fight) _____ about the dog last week.

   Jerry and Bob (fight) _____ about the dog ever since the dog started to dig holes in Jerry's lawn.

PRACTICE 3: Make Sentences

A. Read each sentence. Write a sentence using *ought to*.

1. You should think of your family.

   You ought to think of your family.

2. Lan should thank Tom.

   _____

3. Ed should get a job.

   _____

4. You should tie up your dog.

   _____

5. Everyone should help clean the neighborhood.

   _____

6. Gladys should run for office.

   _____

B. Write a sentence using *ought not to*.

1. You should not have cut in front of the truck.

   You ought not to have cut in front of the truck.

2. Tom should not be unhappy about winning third prize.

   _____

3. Children should not play with matches.

   _____

4. The city should not have a lot of empty houses.

   _____

5. Duke should not quit school and get a job.

   _____

6. You should not fly the flag in the rain.

   _____

PRACTICE 4: Combine Sentences

Make one sentence from two. Use *as*.

1. Molly sat down. Tom walked into the classroom.

   Molly sat down as Tom walked into the classroom.

2. Lewis had a dream. He grew up.

   _____

3. Lan's father watched. Tom opened the car door.

   _____

4. Lan watched. Tom caught some fish.

   _____

5. Paul was driving along the highway. He saw an accident.

   _____

6. She sat in the car. She had time to think.

   _____

PRACTICE 5: Make Questions

Make questions about the underlined word or words. Use *who* or *what*.

1. Your children need a father.

   Who needs a father?

2. Tom brought Lan home.

   _____

3. A bird is singing.

   _____

4. Lan got letters from Viet Nam.

   _____

5. Several cars were parked in front of the house.

   _____

6. The laundry basket is behind the door.

   _____

PRACTICE 1: Verb Tenses

Read the sentence. Write a sentence using the past and *might*.

1. I think I may be able to find another job.

   I thought I might be able to find another job.

2. I think I may get unemployment insurance.

   _____

3. I think I may not come home after work.

   _____

4. My friend says the factory may need someone to repair the machines.

   _____

   _____

5. They say it may rain a lot.

   _____

6. Jake says that he may move.

   _____

7. I think I may not have enough money.

   _____

8. Roy says he may not be able to buy any toys for his sons for Christmas.

   _____

   _____

9. Joyce says she may get a job.

   _____

10. Jimmy says he may be able to make some money cleaning the snow.

    _____

    _____

PRACTICE 2: Verb Forms

Read the sentence. Look at the verb that is given.
Write the verb with *to* or with *-ing*.

1. My job was (take) _to take_ care of the machines.

2. I avoided (tell) _____ my wife the truth.

3. One day Joyce tried (phone) _____ me at work.

4. I had always enjoyed (buy) _____ toys for the boys.

5. I didn't want (worry) _____ her.

6. I was able (get) _____ insurance.

7. I am good at (repair) _____, (clean) _____, and

   (oil) _____ machines.

8. Molly taught her (speak) _____ English.

9. We caught her (take) _____ the money.

10. Lan didn't refuse (go) _____ to California.

11. The neighbors will pay me (clean) _____ the snow off their walks.

12. Little things began (annoy) _____ me.

13. They needed someone (oil and repair) _____ the machines.

14. I might be able (find) _____ another job soon.

15. Last year, business started (slow) _____ down.

PRACTICE 3: Make New Words

Add *un-* to the beginning of the word to make it negative.

1. employed *unemployed*
2. happy _____
3. furnished _____
4. sure _____
5. true _____
6. safe _____
7. seen _____
8. able _____
9. born _____
10. changed _____

11. eaten _____
12. hurt _____
13. marked _____
14. painted _____
15. repaired _____
16. said _____
17. spent _____
18. tested _____
19. told _____
20. zip _____

PRACTICE 4: Make Negative Sentences

Make the sentences negative by using the underlined words with *un-*.

1. Molly is happy.

   Molly is unhappy.

2. The apartment is furnished.

   _____

3. The living room was painted.

   _____

4. She zipped the jacket.

   _____

5. This neighborhood is very safe.

   _____

6. Why is Duke so happy?

   _____

PRACTICE 5: Emphasis

Use *do, does,* or *did* to make the sentence stronger.

1. The employment office sent me to a lot of companies.

   The employment office did send me to a lot of companies.

2. I went to the state employment office.

   _____

3. I want a big, beautiful Christmas tree.

   _____

4. Tran Ty Lan took the tickets.

   _____

5. She gets tired from working all day.

   _____

6. You like him a lot.

   _____

7. They try to help every month.

   _____

8. I made a payment on my car loan.

   _____

9. You want to marry again.

   _____

10. I want a job.

    _____

11. Jackie played with the Dodgers for 10 years.

    _____

12. It feels good to sit down.

    _____

PRACTICE 6: Write a Note

Write a note to your friend. Tell your friend what you have been doing for the past two months.

_____

_____

_____

_____

_____

_____

_____

_____

_____

_____

_____

_____

_____
(Sign your name.)

PRACTICE 7: Listen

Listen to the teacher. Write the words that are missing.

    For 10 years, Roy Johnson took care of _____ machines in _____
                                                     (1)   (2)

small factory. Then he was laid off. He had to find _____ new job. But
                                                                            (3)

_____ new job was very hard to find. Roy read _____ employment
(4)   (5)

ads in _____ paper every day. He went to _____ state employment
               (6)   (7)

office. But nobody could help him find _____ job. He was _____
                                           (8)   (9)

unhappy man.

Note to the teacher: Read the paragraph with normal speed and intonation. Do not pronounce too carefully. Use words in the answer key.

PRACTICE 1: Make New Words

Fill in the boxes with the correct form of the word.
The XXX means there is no word for that box.

	Noun	Adjective	Adverb
1.	freedom	free	freely
2.		blind	
3.	wind		XXX
4.			darkly
5.	happiness		
6.		sick	
7.	dirt		XXX
8.			slowly
9.	lightness		
10.	rain		XXX

PRACTICE 2: Make New Words

Write the correct form of the word in the sentence.
Use the ending -y or the ending -ly.

1. (health)   Ed is a very _healthy_ person.

2. (quick)   The employee did the work _____.

3. (cloud)   It's a _____ day. I think it's going to rain.

4. (awful)   I'm _____ sorry.

5. (quiet)   Ed did his work very _____.

6. (rain)   It's a _____ day. I think I'll stay home.

7. (sharp)   She was angry. She spoke to him _____.

8. (complete)   The house was almost _____ destroyed by fire.

9. (wind)   It's _____. Your hat will blow away.

10. (dirt)   This is a _____ room.

PRACTICE 3: Combine Sentences

Combine the two sentences into one. Use *who* or *which*.

1. Garcia said he was glad no one was hurt. Garcia lives at 105 Maple Avenue.

   Garcia, who lives at 105 Maple Avenue, said he was glad no one was hurt.

2. The section of the newspaper has only ads. The section is the classified ad section.

   _____

   _____

3. The accident was caused by a truck. The truck was unable to make the sharp turn at the bottom of Hill Street.

   _____

   _____

4. Two houses were almost destroyed. The houses are at the corner of Hill St. and Maple Ave.

   _____

   _____

5. The house on Maple Ave. was empty. The house belongs to Center City Land Company.

   _____

   _____

6. Mary Garcia told reporters what she saw. Mary Garcia lives at 105 Maple Ave.

   _____

   _____

7. The cat is free to a good home. The cat is a two-year-old female.

   _____

   _____

8. Terry's needs a cook. The cook must be experienced and fast.

   _____

   _____

PRACTICE 4: Combine Sentences

Make sentences using *not only . . . but also.*

1. Dogs dig up the lawns. They mess up the sidewalks.

   Not only do dogs dig up the lawns, but they also mess up the sidewalks.

2. I clean the machines. I oil and repair them.

   _____

   _____

3. The news is on Channel 3. The news is on Channel 5 and Channel 9.

   _____

   _____

4. Unemployed people smoke and drink more. They hit their children more.

   _____

   _____

5. You should talk to your family. You should tell the children the truth.

   _____

   _____

6. He bought some toys for the children. He bought them some clothes.

   _____

   _____

7. To get an apartment you have to read the ads. You have to make a lot of telephone calls.

   _____

   _____

additional	(a di' shun ul)

PRACTICE 5: Write a Classified Ad

Write a classified ad to put in the newspaper. Your ad can be about something you lost or something you found. Or you can write an ad about something you want to sell or buy.

Make the ad about 20 words. (There is one price for the first 20 words. You will have to pay more for each additional word.)

Your Ad: _____

_____

_____

_____

_____

_____

_____

Name: _____

Address: _____

_____

Phone: (_____) _____

$4.40 for the first 20 words. $0.20 for each additional word.
Send your check or money order with your ad. Send to:

THE CENTER CITY NEWS
7 Hill Street
Center City, New York 13202

1. How many words did you write? _____

2. How much will your ad cost? _____

PRACTICE 6: Story with Missing Words

Write the missing words.

Being Out of Work Can Make You Sick

Unemployment and health problems go together. This was the finding of a _____ study by the Center for Work _____ Mental Health in Washington, D.C.

Doctors _____ the country took part in the _____. Information from them showed more sickness _____ places where many people are out _____ work. The study found that unemployed _____ smoke and drink more. They hit _____ children more. And they have more _____ fights.

"People show they are under _____ in different ways," says the study _____. "Some get sick. Others become angry _____ depressed. They drink too much or _____ violent."

Two out of every four _____ workers at one factory reported that _____ could not sleep. Others said they _____ not eat or got sick when _____ did. These are signs of mental _____.

According to the study, most people _____ stand a few weeks of unemployment _____ health problems. The hardest time comes _____ six months when unemployment insurance stops. _____ a year, unemployed workers often feel _____ hopeless that they stop looking for _____ job.

If you are unemployed, what _____ you do to avoid health problems? _____ at the Center for Work and _____ Health give these answers.

You are _____ sure to feel angry and depressed. _____ you should not keep these feelings _____ yourself. Bring them out in the open.

PRACTICE 1: Answer Questions

Answer the questions using *because*.

1. Why don't you throw the rude man off the bus?

    I don't throw him off the bus, because he doesn't bother me.

2. Why didn't Chris ride to school with her parents?

    _____

    _____

3. Why did Chris bake some cookies?

    _____

    _____

4. Why should everyone learn how to cook?

    _____

    _____

5. Why was Mrs. Mitchell glad that she went to the open house at school?

    _____

    _____

    _____

6. Why do many people buy insurance?

    _____

    _____

7. Why did Ray take aspirin?

    _____

    _____

8. Why was Chris late last night?

    _____

    _____

correct   (cor ect′)

PRACTICE 2: Correct the Errors

Read the sentences. Correct anything that is not right.
Write the sentence correctly.

1. I use to watch him as the passengers get on the bus.

   I used to watch him as the passengers got on the bus.

2. There weren't much passengers on the bus.

   _____

3. Tell me where is the book.

   _____

4. We are living in Center City for the last three years.

   _____

   _____

5. Why you don't throw that rude man off the bus?

   _____

   _____

6. The bell will ring when the program will be ready to begin.

   _____

   _____

7. Michael went with his mother so he wanted to see the machine shop.

   _____

   _____

8. The Mitchells heard the bell to ring.

   _____

9. Some girls don't like chemistry, and I do.

   _____

Note to the teacher: Instead of rewriting the sentence, the student may cross
                    out what is incorrect and write the correction above it.

PRACTICE 3: Make Questions

Make questions using *What about* and the words given.

1. the dog and the moon

   What about the dog and the moon?

2. baking some cookies

   _____

3. asking her younger brother

   _____

4. the Mitchell family

   _____

5. the open house at school

   _____

6. a cup of coffee

   _____

PRACTICE 4: Answer Questions

Answer each question, using one of these answers: *OK. Sure. That would be nice.*
Can you think of other answers?

1. What about going home? ___ *OK.* _____

2. What about asking Chris? _____

3. What about sitting right here? _____

4. What about watching TV? _____

5. What about taking the bus? _____

6. What about a cup of coffee? _____

PRACTICE 5: Make New Words

Read the sentence. Then write what the person is.

1. He repairs mechanical parts   *He's an auto mechanic.*
   on autos.

2. He drives a bus.   _____

3. She teaches school.   _____

4. He plays basketball.   _____

5. She coaches basketball.   _____

6. He edits the newspaper.   _____

7. They manage the apartment.   _____

8. He drives a truck.   _____

9. They fight fires.   _____

10. He grows apples.   _____

PRACTICE 6: Listen

Circle the letter of the sentence that the teacher says.

1. a. I'll give them the bicycle.

   b. I'll give him the bicycle.

2. a. She's a good teacher.

   b. He's a good teacher.

3. a. He's a teacher here.

   b. His teacher's here.

4. a. I heard them open the door.

   b. I heard him open the door.

5. a. She asked him a question.

   b. She asked her a question.

Note to the teacher: In each item read either *a* or *b*. Do not choose the same
letter each time. Do not emphasize the pronouns.

PRACTICE 7: Write a Classified Ad

Some people drive to work together. They share the driving, or they pay the person who drives. These people have a car pool.

Put a classified ad in the newspaper to ask for a car pool. Fill in the information about yourself.

FREE Car Pool Classified Ad

Date: _____

Name: _____

Home Address:

    Street _____

    City _____

Home Phone No.: _____

Work Address:

    Street _____

    City _____

Work Phone No.: _____

Time: I leave home for work at _____

    I leave work for home at _____

[ ] I will share driving.

[ ] I will drive and take _____ riders.

[ ] I need a ride. I do not drive.

Send to:
    Center City Car Pool Ad
    7 Hill Street
    Center City, New York 13202

Lesson 18

PRACTICE 1: Exclamatory Sentences

Use *How* to make a strong sentence.

1. Gene and Gordon were very much alike.

   How much alike Gene and Gordon were!

2. Gordon was happy.

   _____

3. The tale was strange.

   _____

4. Gordon and Gene were gentle.

   _____

5. The Chang family was proud.

   _____

6. It was hard to accept war and killing.

   _____

PRACTICE 2: Prepositions with Verbs

Write *for, up, of, out,* or *near.*

1. They both took care ___of___ hurt animals.

2. They carried _____ wounded soldiers.

3. He looked _____ and saw an enemy standing _____ a wounded man.

4. It's not fair to keep a healthy dog tied _____.

5. Are there any job openings I could apply _____?

6. My unemployment insurance ran _____ in November.

7. Jackie dropped out _____ college when his mother got sick.

PRACTICE 3: Combine Sentences

Combine the two sentences. Use *before* or *after*.

1. Gene and Gordon graduated from high school.
   Their countries called them to war.

   After Gene and Gordon graduated from high school,
   their countries called them to war.

2. Gene went to war. He said good-by to all his friends.

   _____

   _____

3. Gordon went into the armed services. He became a medic.

   _____

   _____

4. The war was over. The men wanted to go home to their families.

   _____

   _____

5. You must cool the cookies for a few minutes. You remove them from the pan.

   _____

   _____

6. Chris had chorus practice at 6:30. She would meet her parents at 7:30.

   _____

   _____

7. We ate dinner. We went into the living room to watch TV.

   _____

   _____

8. Class was over. Tom gave Lan a ride home.

   _____

   _____

PRACTICE 4: Write Sentences

Write sentences using *make the most of* and the words given.

1. (free time) *An unemployed person ought to make the most of his free time.*

2. (day off) _____

3. (new job) _____

4. (summer) _____

5. (trip to Canada) _____

_____

PRACTICE 5: Write Sentences

Read each sentence. Then make a sentence using *above all* to add another idea.

1. Don't avoid telling people that you are out of work.

   Above all, don't give up looking for a job.

2. Talk openly with your family.

   _____

3. When I was out of work, my family was very helpful.

   _____

4. Dogs should be fenced in.

   _____

5. The cook in a snack shop must be fast.

   _____

6. Truck drivers must be over 25.

   _____

PRACTICE 6: Correct the Errors

Read the sentences. Correct anything that is not right.
Write the sentence correctly.

1. I'm awful sorry.

   I'm awfully sorry.

2. The Snack Shop needs a cook which is experienced.

   _____

3. Mrs. King, who's son is a farmer, teach school.

   _____

4. Not only I baked a cake but I make coffee.

   _____

5. I didn't go to school because a cold.

   _____

6. What about bake some cookies?

   _____

7. How Gordon was happy!

   _____

8. Lan should to thank Tom.

   _____

9. Because he went into the living room, he wanted to watch TV.

   _____

   _____

10. Although I had a bad cold, but I went to work.

    _____

    _____

Note to the teacher: Instead of rewriting the sentence, the student may cross
out what is incorrect and write the correction above it.

PRACTICE 7: Story with Missing Words

Write the missing words.

A Strange Tale of War

It was strange how much alike Gene Bridges and Gordon Chang were. When they were young, they both _____ care of hurt animals. They bandaged _____ animals and nursed them back to _____. They enjoyed helping the animals get _____.

Gene Bridges and Gordon Chang both _____ to become doctors so they could _____ people get well. They both learned _____ give first aid. They read many _____ about doctors with great courage. In _____ books they read, doctors gave their _____ and their energy to helping people _____ sickness and danger. Both Gene and _____ longed to be doctors like that.

_____ much alike Gene and Gordon were! _____ seemed to be only one difference _____ them. They lived in different countries _____ opposite sides of the world.

When _____ graduated from high school, it was _____ proud occasion for the Bridges family. _____ was accepted by a college near _____ home. He hoped to work his _____ through college and become a doctor. _____ Chang graduated from high school the _____ year Gene did. It was a _____ occasion for the Chang family, too. _____ was also accepted by a college _____ hoped to become a doctor.

But _____ after Gene and Gordon graduated from _____ school, their countries called them to _____. Before he went off to war, _____ married his girl friend Ginger. Gordon married Grace, the girl he loved.

PRACTICE 1: Write Sentences

Add a sentence about each person.

1. Ed comes from the United States. _He's American._ _____

2. Tom comes from Africa. _____

3. Lan comes from Asia. _____

4. Jill comes from Canada. _____

5. Maria comes from Mexico. _____

6. Lee is from China. _____

7. Hugo comes from Cuba. _____

8. Ran comes from India. _____

PRACTICE 2: Combine Sentences

Combine the two sentences. Use *the more (-er) . . . the more (-er)*.

1. You eat more. You get fatter.

   The more you eat, the fatter you get. _____

2. You speak English better. Other people understand you more.

   _____

3. You read more, you learn more.

   _____

4. The car is bigger. The car is better.

   _____

5. The headline is bigger. The news story is bigger.

   _____

6. There are more people at the party. It is better.

   _____

7. You do your homework faster. You will watch TV sooner.

   _____

PRACTICE 3: Make Sentences

Write a sentence comparing the two things. Use the word given.

1. Asian elephants weigh about 12,000 pounds.
   African elephants weigh about 14,000 pounds.

   A. (large) *African elephants are larger than Asian elephants.*

   B. (small) _____

2. African elephants have two knobs on their trunk.
   Asian elephants have one knob on their trunk.

   A. (more) _____

   _____

   B. (few) _____

   _____

3. African elephants are very hard to train.
   Asian elephants are hard to train.

   A. (hard) _____

   _____

   B. (easy) _____

   _____

4. Ginger spent a lot of money. Kitty didn't spend any money.

   A. (more) _____

   B. (less) _____

5. Ginger weighs 145 pounds. Kitty weighs 125 pounds.

   A. (more) _____

   B. (less) _____

6. Ginger is 24 years old. Kitty is 20 years old.

   A. (old) _____

   B. (young) _____

PRACTICE 4: Write Sentences

Use the words given to make sentences with *if*.

1. (change, need) *If you change doctors, you will need to have a physical exam.*

2. (find, give) _____

_____

3. (have enough money, buy) _____

_____

4. (wake up early, call) _____

_____

5. (have time, clean) _____

_____

6. (have questions, ask) _____

_____

7. (lose my job, look for) _____

_____

8. (register, vote) _____

_____

9. (can afford, buy) _____

_____

10. (watch TV, fall asleep) _____

_____

PRACTICE 5: Fill in the Blank

Choose the correct word to complete the sentences.

although	because	so	when
as	if		where

1. It is important to have a complete physical exam ___*if*___ you are changing doctors.

2. _____ you breathe deeply and cough, the doctor will listen to sounds in your heart and chest.

3. How can you find out about free clinics _____ you live?

4. _____ you telephone the doctor, ask if there is anything you should bring.

5. You should have a physical exam _____ you may feel very healthy.

6. I'm going to have a physical exam _____ I have been getting bad headaches.

7. Ed's back hurt a lot, _____ he made an appointment with his doctor.

8. _____ you have any questions during your physical exam, ask the doctor.

9. _____ I have headaches, I take aspirins.

10. I'm going to buy a newspaper, _____ I can check the classified ads for an apartment.

PRACTICE 6: Correct the Errors

There are 11 words that have an -*s* or -*es* missing. Can you find all of them?
Add the -*s* or -*es*.

Ann has given two English book to Ed. He know he has to give the two book back to her after he finish reading them. Ed want to read the book and to have his two son read them, too. He know they will learn a lot of thing from reading the book and asking question about them.

PRACTICE 7: Make Sentences Passive

Change the sentences to the passive. Begin with the underlined word.

1. We often call <u>animals</u> dumb because they cannot talk.

   Animals are often called dumb because they cannot talk.

2. We can train <u>elephants</u> to do many things.

   _____

3. We use <u>elephants</u> as work animals.

   _____

4. We can sell <u>elephant tusks</u> for a lot of money.

   _____

   _____

5. Men are still killing <u>elephants</u> although there are laws against such killings.

   _____

   _____

6. We have trained <u>elephants</u> to work in shows.

   _____

PRACTICE 8: Write Sentences with *get*

Write sentences with the words given. Use *get* in the present or past tense.

1. get beaten *Our baseball team got beaten yesterday.* _____

2. get married _____

3. get paid _____

4. get caught _____

5. get picked _____

6. get drunk _____

PRACTICE 1: Finish the Sentences

Read the sentences. Add an idea using *but*.

1. I took exams in every subject *but math and writing.*

2. I went to every store _____

3. I invited all my friends _____

4. Everyone came to the party _____

5. Everyone worked late _____

6. All my friends know how to run a computer _____

PRACTICE 2: Prepositions

Write *in, on,* or *at* in the sentence.

1. Jackie Robinson was the first black player ___*in*___ the major leagues.

2. Jackie was born _____ the South _____ 1919.

3. Some players _____ his own team would not talk to him.

4. Some games were played _____ night.

5. His record _____ sports gave him a chance to go to the University of California.

6. _____ what day of the week does Christmas come _____ 2000?

7. The game begins _____ 7 o'clock.

8. She writes _____ the paper with a pencil.

9. Jim Parker lives _____ 140 Main Street.

10. The teacher is standing _____ her desk.

PRACTICE 3: Correct the Errors

Read the sentences. Correct anything that is not right.
Write the sentence correctly.

1. News storys give the facts about things that has happened in your city.

   News stories give the facts about things that have happened in your city.

2. This is the six accident there in two year.

   _____

3. Don't avoid to tell people you are out of work.

   _____

4. I am living here for the last three months.

   _____

5. Don't give up to look for job.

   _____

6. I will help you if you will need help.

   _____

7. She was disappointing at me.

   _____

8. The another students began to arrive for class.

   _____

9. Which U.S. president was borned in February 22?

   _____

10. People who gets a newspaper mainly for sports turns to the sports section first.

    _____

    _____

Note to the teacher: Instead of rewriting the sentence, the student may cross
out what is incorrect and write the correction above it.

% (per cent)	expense

PRACTICE 4: Read a Pie Chart

Don Miller is taking a course on living with a budget. His teacher said, "Before you can make a budget, you should know how you are spending your money right now."

Don made this pie chart to show how he spends his money. (In a pie chart, everything adds up to 100%.)

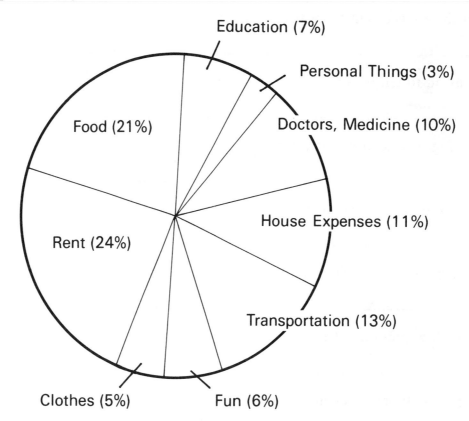

A. Find the answers by looking at the pie chart. You may give short answers.

1. What does most of Don Miller's money go for? _____

2. How much of his money does Don spend on clothes? _____

3. What per cent of his money does Don spend on having fun? _____

4. Does Don spend more on education or on clothes? _____

5. Does Don spend more on house expenses or on transportation? _____

6. Teachers of budget-making say you shouldn't spend more than 25% of your monthly pay for rent. Is Don spending too much for rent, or is his spending just about right?

_____

7. Is Don putting any money into savings? _____

PRACTICE 4: continued

B. Think about how you spend your money. Is it the same as Don Miller or different? Write sentences about yourself. Use the words given.

1. (rent and food) _Most of my money goes for rent and food._

2. (doctors and medicine) _____

_____

3. (education) _____

_____

4. (transportation) _____

_____

5. (clothing) _____

_____

6. (about 25%) _____

_____

7. (having fun) _____

_____

C. Almost all of us wish we had more money. Write 5 things you would do if you had more money.

1. _I would give more money to my church if I had a lot of money._

2. _____

_____

3. _____

_____

4. _____

_____

5. _____

_____

6. _____

PRACTICE 5: Listen

Circle the letter of the sentence that the teacher says.

1. a. You can afford an apartment.

   b. You can't afford an apartment.

2. a. Kitty can swim.

   b. Kitty can't swim.

3. a. She can find things to do.

   b. She can't find things to do.

4. a. My family can afford a tutor.

   b. My family can't afford a tutor.

5. a. You can go out alone at night.

   b. You can't go out alone at night.

6. a. Ginger can speak English.

   b. Ginger can't speak English.

7. a. Elephants can learn to stand on their heads.

   b. Elephants can't learn to stand on their heads.

8. a. O'Toole can climb the building.

   b. O'Toole can't climb the building.

Note to the teacher: In each item read *a* or *b*. Do not choose the same letter each time. Do not emphasize *can* or *can't*.

central (cen′ trul)   modern (mod′ ern)   pizza (pēt′ su)

PRACTICE 1: Alphabetical Order

A telephone directory has names of people and businesses in alphabetical order.

Words beginning with the letters *a* to *e* are in the first third of the directory. Words beginning with *f* through *p* are in the middle third. And words beginning with *q* through *z* are in the last third of the directory.

Tell whether the people and businesses given are in the first (1), second (2), or third (3) part of the directory. Do not alphabetize by the word *the*.

1. Central Business School   *1*
2. The Modern Shoe Shop   *2*
3. Indian River Fruit Store   _____
4. The York Street Pet Shop   _____
5. Ann's Hat Shop   _____
6. The Pizza Place   _____
7. Valley Utility Company   _____
8. Lake Charlotte High School   _____
9. The Bakery   _____
10. Chang's Asian Food Shop   _____

PRACTICE 2: Make an Alphabetical List

Central High School needs a directory of its English teachers. Make an alphabetical list by the last name of the teachers.

Dr. Ann Fisher   1. *Dr. John Buck* _____

Mr. Fred Miller   2. _____

Ms. Molly Smith   3. _____

Dr. John Buck   4. _____

Mr. Ned Johnson   5. _____

Ms. Judy Chan   6. _____

Mr. Carlos Lopez   7. _____

PRACTICE 3: Write Questions and Answers

Write a question asking about the meaning of the word. Then answer the
question. Look up the word in the dictionary if you don't know its meaning.

1. weight _What does weight mean ?_
   Weight means how heavy something is.

2. weekly

   _____

   _____

3. guide

   _____

   _____

4. improve

   _____

   _____

5. speed

   _____

   _____

6. physician

   _____

   _____

PRACTICE 4: Make New Words

Fill in the boxes with the correct form of the word.
The XXX means there is no word for that box.

	Noun	Adjective	Adverb
1.	strangeness	strange	strangely
2.		healthy	healthily
3.			sadly
4.	safety		
5.		fair	
6.	poor		
7.		snowy	XXX
8.	gladness		
9.			openly
10.		painful	

PRACTICE 5: Make Questions with *whose*

Make questions about the underlined words. Use *whose*.

1. Hugh's cousins were at the reunion.

   Whose cousins were at the reunion ?

2. Michael's medicine is on the table.

   _____

3. Tom gave Lan's family some fish.

   _____

4. Jack's car got hit from behind.

   _____

5. This is Ginger's book.

   _____

6. Gene's mother is in the hospital.

   _____

PRACTICE 6: Repeat Words for Emphasis

Use the underlined word two times to make a strong sentence.

1. Jobs today take <u>more</u> education.

   Jobs today take more and more education.

2. The days are getting <u>longer</u>.

3. She said his name <u>over</u>.

4. I read the letter <u>again</u>.

5. I'm feeling <u>better</u> every day.

6. Today <u>more</u> people are learning to use computers.

PRACTICE 7: *to, too,* and *two*

Write *to, too,* or *two* in the sentences.

1. The Johnsons have _*two*_ sons.

2. Ann wants _____ live in Center City.

3. My wife eats a lot of fish, and I do, _____.

4. Ed goes _____ work early. Tom does, _____.

5. Duke is 16. He's _____ young _____ drink beer.

6. We need _____ people _____ help us.

7. _____ find the word *weigh* in the dictionary, turn _____ pages showing words that begin with *w.*

PRACTICE 8: Listen

Circle the letter of the sentence the teacher says.

1. a. Your teacher is in room 302.

   b. You're the teacher in room 302.

2. a. Who's in the kitchen?

   b. Whose kitchen is this?

3. a. He's watching TV.

   b. She's watching TV.

4. a. Jack gave him the money.

   b. Jack gave them the money.

5. a. Jane's an interested person.

   b. Jane's an interesting person.

6. a. He's worked here 14 years.

   b. He's worked here 40 years.

7. a. Ellen is 16.

   b. Ellen is 60.

Note to the teacher: In each item read *a* or *b*. Do not choose the same letter
each time. Do not emphasize the difference between the pairs
of sentences.

PRACTICE 1: Make New Words

Read the sentence. Write what the person is.

1. He trades fur. _He's a fur trader._

2. He works in a factory. _____

3. He does research on cancer. _____

4. She's a student in high school. _____

5. She reports in the newspaper. _____

6. She trains dogs. _____

7. They own a home. _____

8. They grow trees. _____

9. He has a cotton farm. _____

10. She teaches in a college. _____

PRACTICE 2: they're, their, and there

Write *they're, their,* or *there* in the sentences.

1. The Millers are proud of _their_ children.

2. Put the book over _____.

3. _____ son is a school teacher.

4. _____ discussing adult education.

5. Kitty's parents like to visit her in her new apartment. _____ going

_____ tonight.

6. _____ going home.

7. Slaves often took _____ owner's last name.

8. Your coat is _____ on the sofa.

PRACTICE 3: *make, take,* and *do*

Write the correct form of *make, take* or *do* in the sentences.

1. Ed _made_ an appointment with the doctor.

2. It _____ ten minutes to walk to school.

3. I always _____ my time when I eat my meals.

4. Duke _____ his math lesson at Mr. Newman's house last night.

5. Yesterday he _____ a date with Ginger to go to the movies.

6. Sam _____ notes in his notebook as he listens to the teacher.

PRACTICE 4: Word Order in Sentences

Add the word to the sentences.

1. (big) Terry avoided the highways between cities.

   Terry avoided the big highways between cities.

2. (out) At each town, the people came to cheer him.

   _____

3. (and weaker) As Terry ran into Ontario, he got weaker.

   _____

   _____

4. (still) Terry's Marathon of Hope was inspiring all of Canada.

   _____

   _____

5. (with him) Sometimes, people joined Terry and ran a few miles to cheer him on.

   _____

   _____

6. (funny) He told stories when friends came to visit.

   _____

   _____

PRACTICE 5: Correct the Errors

Read the sentences. Correct anything that is not right.
Write the sentence correctly.

1. Ann is very well swimmer.

   Ann is a very good swimmer.

2. Jake will never move off the woods.

3. The neighbors are proud with their clean parks.

4. It's no safe to play with matches.

5. Sam has new fine watch.

6. Paul could hardly see the road, couldn't he?

7. Didn't you forgot anything?

8. Tom catched a cold last week.

9. (What's your sister like?)
   She likes to go camping.

Note to the teacher: Instead of rewriting the sentence, the student may cross out what is incorrect and write the correction above it.

In item 9, only the answer is to be corrected.

PRACTICE 6: Sentence Order

Put the sentences in the right order to make a story. First, number them in the right order.

_____ George Carver was born in 1864.

_____ First he went to Simpson College and later to Iowa State University.

_____ He wanted to go to college but had to wait three years.

_____ He lived with the Carvers on their farm.

_____ When he was 22, he graduated with honors from high school.

_____ When George was about 12, he left the farm to go to school.

Now write the sentences. (Do not write the numbers.)

_____

_____

_____

_____

_____

_____

_____

_____

_____

_____

_____

_____

_____

Note to the teacher: Have the student read the sentences aloud in his numbered order before he writes them out. This will help him determine if his order is correct.

elevator (el u vā′ tor)   jeans   lane

PRACTICE 1: Answer Questions

Answer the question using *must not* or *not permitted*. Then write another sentence that adds another idea.

1. I'm 17. Can I drink beer?

No, *you must not. You're too young.* _____

2. Can I wear blue jeans to school?

No, _____

3. Can I eat in my bedroom?

No, _____

4. Can we use the elevator if there is a fire?

No, _____

5. Can we smoke in this building?

No, _____

6. Can I use this telephone to call India?

No, _____

7. Can I buy this medicine without a prescription?

No, _____

8. Can I park my car for a few minutes in the fire lane?

No, _____

9. Can anyone park in a place for the handicapped?

No, _____

PRACTICE 2: Sentence Order

Put the sentences in the right order to make a story. First, number them in the right order.

_____ They did not see the Pacific Ocean until Nov. 7, 1805.

_____ In 1803, President Thomas Jefferson bought the Louisiana Territory from the French.

_____ They left St. Louis in May of 1804 and started up the Missouri River.

_____ Sacajawea was their guide.

_____ Jefferson picked Lewis and Clark to explore the territory.

_____ It was a huge, wild country.

Now write the sentences. (Do not write the numbers.)

_____

_____

_____

_____

_____

_____

_____

_____

_____

_____

_____

_____

Note to the teacher: Have the student read the sentences aloud in his numbered order before he writes them out. This will help him determine if his order is correct.

PRACTICE 3: Combine Sentences

Combine the sentences. Use *unless*.

1. They could not reach the Pacific Ocean. Friendly Indians helped them.

   They could not reach the Pacific Ocean unless friendly Indians helped them.

2. We have a guide. We will never reach the Pacific Ocean.

   _____

3. Captain Lewis would not hire Charbonneau. Sacajawea, his wife, went along.

   _____

   _____

4. The Shoshonis would not have welcomed Lewis and Clark. Sacajawea was with them.

   _____

   _____

5. The men on the expedition would die. They ate the horses.

   _____

PRACTICE 4: Correct the Errors

In the paragraph below, 17 words need capital letters. Two of them have been found. Can you find the other 15? Write the capital letters.

      T   A

The "Apostle to the illiterates," frank laubach, was an international missionary, who traveled to more than 100 countries in asia, africa, north america, south america, and europe. dr. laubach helped start literacy programs in more than 300 languages. he inspired many thousands of teachers. several years ago, *life* magazine said that more than 60 million people had become literate because of him.

PRACTICE 5: Word Order in Sentences

Put the words in the right order to make a sentence.

1. no she were ate berries the There so off bark trees the

   There were no berries so she ate the bark off the trees.

2. St. Louis were got Lewis they Clark to heroes and when back

   _____

   _____

3. twenties Some in died people that 1812 in claim she her

   _____

4. hardest months The journey part the of in next came two the

   _____

5. American No honored been so statues other woman has by many

   _____

   _____

PRACTICE 6: Listen

Listen to the teacher. Write the missing words.

Sacajawea played _____ important part _____ _____ Lewis
                    (1)   (2)   (3)

and Clark expedition. She made life easier _____ _____ men. She looked
                                              (4)   (5)

_____ roots and berries. Sacajawea also sewed clothes _____ _____
   (6)   (7)   (8)

men and caught fish _____ their meals. On _____ expeditions, she warned
                       (9)   (10)

_____ men _____ many dangerous things. She will always have _____
   (11)   (12)   (13)

special place _____ American history.
                 (14)

Note to the teacher: Do not pronounce the missing words carefully or in an
                     exaggerated fashion. Say the sentences with natural speed and
                     intonation. The missing words can be found in the answer key.

PRACTICE 7: Story with Missing Words

Write the missing words.

Frank C. Laubach
Among the Maranaos

A small hot room was crowded with men and women, all dressed in brightly colored clothes. These people were Maranaos. The Maranaos _____ Muslims who lived on a big _____ in the south of the Philippines.

_____ important meeting was ready to start. _____ men were sitting at a table _____ the front of the room. One _____ the men was a chief of Lanao Province. _____ was a very powerful chief. You _____ tell that just by looking at _____. This Muslim chief was about five _____ a half feet tall, with flashing _____ eyes. A long dagger was in _____ belt.

The other man at the _____ was only a little taller than _____ chief. This man was an American _____. He had light blue eyes and _____ kind smile. But that day his _____ seemed sad.

This missionary was Frank _____ Laubach.

The missionary stood up and _____ to speak. "My friends," Dr. Laubach _____ in the Maranao language. He was _____ learning to speak Maranao, so he _____ very slowly.

"My friends," Dr. Laubach _____, "with our lessons, thousands of people _____ Lanao have learned to read and _____ Maranao. Our teachers have taught them _____ the market places and in their _____. Now, mothers are reading books about _____ care. Farmers are reading books about better farming."

Answer Keys

Note: In some cases, there is more than one possible answer. Accept all correct answers from your students.

LESSON 1

Practice 1
1. —
2. taxes
3. boxes
4. classes
5. businesses
6. Computers
7. machine, names, addresses
8. milk

Practice 2
1. —
2. into
3. in
4. for
5. of
6. at
7. in
8. in
9. of
10. in
11. for
12. in, at

Practice 3
1. —
2. This machine works much faster than a human.
3. They help to make paper, cars, TVs, and many other things.
4. Computers help you to telephone other places quickly.
5. You can play these games on your own TV.
6. Some computers do just one job.
7. It may be as little as a radio.
8. Computers tell us if a person is very sick.

Practice 4
Answers will vary.

Practice 5
1. —
2. used
3. trained
4. used
5. read
6. made
7. dropped
8. trained

Practice 6
1. —
2. Computers are used at home.
3. Computers are used to build airplanes.
4. Money can be stolen from banks (by computer).
5. Some business forms can be read (by computers).
6. Computers will be used in businesses and at home.

Practice 7
1. —
2. Does a person use computers at home?
3. Can people steal money from banks by computer?
4. Do some computers do just one job?
5. Will people use computers at home?
6. Did Carla have two English classes today?
7. Did Gail pay her telephone bill?
8. Was Gail's uncle taking pictures at the wedding?
9. Is Miller the man wearing the yellow shirt?
10. Has Jason had lunch?

Practice 8
Answers will vary.

Practice 9
Answers will vary.

LESSON 2

Practice 1
1. —
2. —
3. fastest
4. cheapest
5. saddest
6. largest
7. highest
8. lightest
9. biggest
10. happiest
11. prettiest
12. best

Practice 2
1. —
2. youngest
3. fastest
4. cheapest
5. brightest
6. best
7. saddest
8. largest
9. hottest
10. prettiest

Practice 3
1. —
2. came
3. planned
4. argued
5. went
6. died
7. choked, ate
8. told
9. broke
10. cut
11. ate
12. made

Practice 4
1. —
2. have lived
3. has worked
4. has lived
5. have played
6. hasn't eaten
7. haven't rescued
8. have used
9. have lived
10. have driven
11. has written
12. haven't given

Practice 5
1. —
2. Someone
3. anyone
4. anyone
5. someone
6. Someone

Practice 6-A and 6-B
Answers will vary.

Practice 7
1. —
2. Yes, it is.
3. No, I wasn't.
4. No, I haven't.
5. Yes, they do.
6. Yes, he did.
7. Yes, they can. (Yes, he can.)
8. No, he doesn't.
9. Yes, she (he) is.
10. Yes, they will.
11. No, they haven't.
12. Yes, they are.
13. No, no one will. (No, they won't.)
14. Yes, anyone can.
15. Yes, you are.
16. No, they can't.

Practice 8
See page 9 in *Skill Book 4*.

LESSON 3

Practice 1
1. —
2. No, she doesn't live by herself.
3. No, he doesn't live by himself.
4. Yes, he was cleaning it by himself.
5. Yes, I go by myself.
6. Yes, she was there by herself.

Practice 2
1. —
2. to live
3. give
4. to swim
5. take
6. to see

Practice 3
1. —
2. Let's ask them to dinner soon.
3. Ads can help you find apartments for rent.
4. Write short answers to the questions.
5. What costs did Jane and Kitty share?
6. Why did Kitty want her own apartment?

Practice 4
1. —
2. isn't she?
3. is there?
4. don't they?
5. hasn't she?
6. isn't it?
7. wasn't he?
8. don't they?
9. don't you?
10. will she?

Practice 5
1. —
2. up
3. for
4. for
5. up
6. to
7. for
8. with
9. up
10. with
11. to
12. in
13. up
14. to
15. in

Practice 6
1. —
2. other
3. another
4. another
5. Other
6. Others
7. another
8. other
9. another
10. another
11. other
12. another

Practice 7
1. you
2. to
3. you
4. a
5. you
6. of

Practice 8
1. One person
2. Yes
3. O'Toole
4. Kitty
5. 12 Garden St. Center City, N.Y. 13202
6. 105 Parkview St., Apt. No. 307 Center City, N.Y. 13207
7. 4/30/87
8. 4/30/87
9. Kitty O'Toole (signed)

LESSON 4

Practice 1 and 2
Answers will vary.

Practice 3
1. —
2. Don't let the flag touch the floor.
3. The apartment was not in a safe part of the city.
4. Let's not quit for today.
5. Let's not ask them to dinner.
6. Flag Day in the United States is not on June 15.
7. The stars on the U. S. flag are not red.

Practice 4
1. —
2. It's OK not to ask Ann in the morning.
3. It's great not to get up early in the morning.
4. It's rude not to salute.
5. It's rude for a man not to remove his hat.

Practice 5
1. —
2. The top left corner of the flag is blue.
3. The red maple leaf stands for the country of Canada.
4. It's rude for a man not to remove his hat for his country's flag.
5. There were 22 safe, clean apartments in the building.
6. There was a large, clean eat-in kitchen in the apartment.

Practice 6
Answers will vary.

Practice 7
See page 23 in *Skill Book 4*

LESSON 5

Practice 1
1. —	6. up	11. from
2. up	7. by, on	12. up
3. for	8. at	13. at
4. at	9. for	14. on
5. for	10. up	15. by

Practice 2
Answers will vary.

Practice 3
A. a, The, the, X, the, The, X, the, The, the, a
B. X, an, the, X, the, an, a, a, The, a, the
C. the, the, The, a, X, X, X, X, X, X, A, a, the, a

Practice 4
1. —
2. Judy worked until her baby was born.
3. She worked until she became tired.
4. Write until I tell you to stop.
5. Sit here until someone calls your name.
6. She was in the water until I rescued her.
7. He didn't say anything until dinner was over.
8. They worked hard on the sewers until they were clean.

9. We will stay until the fireworks are over.
10. Judy stayed home with the children until they went to school.
11. Kitty looked for apartments until she got tired.
12. We are going to sit in the car until it's time to go in the house.

Practice 5
See page 29 in *Skill Book 4*

LESSON 6

Practice 1
1. —
2. yourself
3. herself
4. myself
5. yourself
6. himself

Practice 2
1. —
2. He did well enough in his other classes.
3. Duke knew Mr. Newman from church camp.
4. I'll be 16 next Tuesday.
5. Duke just needed some help.
6. Duke started doing his math lessons at school, too.
7. You did most of it yourself.
8. Mr. Newman never made Duke feel stupid.

Practice 3
1. —
2. Duke asked to speak to Jack Newman, who ran the press room.
3. Jack believed that Duke needed some help.
4. They give services to people who live in the city.
5. I will not be poor when I grow up.
6. He loves me, and I love him.
7. I will have a fine car when I grow up.
8. Sometimes when I stay up late, I play my radio quietly.
9. Lewis was 20 when he met Judy.
10. Although they had enough money to live on, they didn't own their own home.
11. A computer is a machine that works with facts like names and addresses.

Practice 4
Answers will vary.

Practice 5
Answers will vary.

Practice 6
See page 35 in *Skill Book 4.*

LESSON 7

Practice 1
1. —	5. is
2. is	6. are
3. is	7. is
4. is	8. are

Practice 2
1. —	5. too
2. to	6. too
3. too	7. to
4. to	8. too

Practice 3
1. —
2. What did Mrs. Hoover tell the police?
3. Where did the fire department rescue Mike O'Toole from?
4. When will O'Toole begin his climb?
5. What did the Lions Club agree to do?
6. Where can tutors get application forms (from)?
7. Who (whom) did Mike Romano speak for?
8. What did she thank the tutors for?
9. When did Lewis die?
10. Where did the fire fighters carry the rope?

Practice 4
1. —
2. The young singer left his three sports cars to his cousin, Luke Jones, who led Lewis's band.
3. "This city needs a better zoo," said Hugh Baker, (who is) the public information officer for the Huron City Zoo.
4. Lewis left his shares to his aunt, Judy Jones, who raised him after his parents died.
5. O'Toole, who says that he is a human fly, was trying to climb the side of the Union Building.
6. Dr. Mary Luther, (who is) president of the school board, was the main speaker of the evening.

Practice 5
1. —
2. The hearings will be open to the public.
3. Lewis died at the age of 27 last year.
4. Lewis left his home in Florida to his grandmother and grandfather.
5. Every week 5,000 people go to the zoo.
6. You have each helped a student in math or reading.
7. Mr. and Mrs. Hoover's apartment was broken into yesterday afternoon.
8. The children tell me that they like the zoo a lot.

Practice 6
1. —
2. People were so amused that they laughed at Mike O'Toole.
3. His music was so good that it won him four gold records.
4. So many people spoke at the hearings that they had to be continued on another day.
5. Duke felt so blue about getting an *F* in math that he wanted to quit school.

Practice 7
Answers should match the sentences read by the teacher.

LESSON 8

Practice 1
1. — 3. no 5. no
2. not 4. not 6. not

Practice 2
1. — 7. when
2. why 8. when
3. which, which 9. where
4. why 10. what
5. which 11. where
6. when 12. when

Practice 3
Jake Bush lived alone in the woods. Jake went to the store only a few times a year. He went there to buy coffee, sugar, fish hooks, and a few other things. There was only one way from Jake's home in the hills to the store. And that way was 15 miles each way on foot.

Practice 4
1. —
2. He was hardly ever sick.
3. Jake hardly ever went to the store.
4. Duke is hardly ever late.
5. He hardly ever speaks to anyone.
6. Jake hardly ever asks anyone for help.
7. Ann is hardly ever sad.

Practice 5
1. —
2. Hugh's family hardly ever gets together, do they?
3. Jake was hardly ever sick, was he?
4. Jake hardly ever went to the store, did he?
5. Kitty and her roommate hardly ever stay home from work, do they?
6. Ann is hardly ever sad, is she?
7. Sam hardly ever speaks to Jim, does he?
8. She hardly ever baked a cake for him, did she?

Practice 6
1. —
2. can 4. can
   could could
3. can 5. can
   could could

Practice 7
Answers will vary.

Practice 8
See page 47 in *Skill Book 4*.

LESSON 9

Practice 1
1. —
2. on 6. out
3. over 7. up
4. up 8. on
5. up, up 9. out of

Practice 2
1. — 5. for
2. for 6. since
3. since 7. since
4. for 8. for

Practice 3-A
1. —
2. 12 (next to Fran's Sports Center)
3. At the Pet Shop (8)
4. At Rings and Things (9)
5. At the Coffee Shop (13)
6. At Fran's Sports Center (14)
7. At Jack's Fix-It (15)
8. At the Read-More Book Store (4)
9. 20 (next to the Shoe Outlet)
10. 11 (next to Rings and Things)

Practice 3-B
Answers will vary.

Practice 4
1. —
2. Many owners of houses said they had no money.
3. A large group of South Side Neighbors went to a city council meeting.
4. Fix them up instead!
5. Our old people are afraid to go out!
6. They were proud of their clean streets and parks.

Practice 5
1. —
2. someone 5. Some
3. Someone 6. some
4. anything 7. anything

Practice 6, 7 and 8
Answers will vary.

Practice 9
Answers should match the sentences read by the teacher.

LESSON 10

Practice 1 and 2
Answers will vary.

Practice 3
1. —
2. Mrs. Brown knows how to bake an apple pie.
3. The clowns know how to make the crowd laugh.
4. Jake knew how to cure himself.
5. Sam learned how to live in the woods.
6. The tutors know how to help students in reading and math.
7. She learned how to speak in public.

Practice 4
Answers will vary.

Practice 5
(Some sentences have two possible answers.)
1. —
2. —
3. He learned how easy it was to ride a horse.
4. We know how happy the clowns make the crowd.
5. Sue and Tom know how exciting the rides are.
6. We can tell how proud Sue is of her horse.
   (We can tell how proud of her horse Sue is.)

7. He knows how far it is from here to Sugar Hill.
   (He knows how far from here to Sugar Hill it is.)
8. We watched how hard it was for the tractor to pull against the machine.
9. Tom showed how unhappy he was not to win first prize.
10. No one knows how interested Duke is in sports.
    (No one knows how interested in sports Duke is.)

Practice 6
A. 2,490,000
   415,000
   20,750
   15,200
   60,200,000
B. six hundred ninety thousand
   five thousand
   three hundred thousand five hundred
   one million
   one hundred thousand
   twenty three thousand six hundred
   seven hundred twenty-two

Practice 7
The second part of the answer will vary.
Possible answers are given.
1. —
2. That's easy for you to say.
   You're a math teacher.
3. That's easy for you to say.
   You're a bus driver.
4. That's easy for you to say.
   You know English very well.
5. That's easy for you to say.
   You're a good swimmer.
6. That's easy for you to say.
   You know how to ride a horse.

Practice 8
See page 61 and 62 in *Skill Book 4.*

LESSON 11

Practice 1
1. —
2. Would you let me watch you carve something?
3. Would you let us (me) borrow money for home repairs?
4. Would you watch the fireworks with us (me)?
5. Would you run for the city council?
6. Would you tell the story to the newspapers?

Practice 2 and 3
Answers will vary.

Practice 4
— was living
— discussed, are not allowed, will have
— had said
— frowned, said, have been living, telling
— answered, know, will want
— got, moving, will have

Practice 5
1. — 4. not
2. not 5. no
3. no 6. not

Practice 6
1. —
2. the
3. the, a, the
4. The, a, a, the
5. an, the (a)
6. an
7. a, the
8. the, a
9. An
10. the, the, the, a (the)
11. The
12. The, the

Practice 7
Answers will vary.

Practice 8
1. lives	5. is
2. wants	6. want
3. say	7. will
4. has	8. am staying

LESSON 12

Practice 1
1. —
2. The fire started in a big, empty house.
3. Your dog has made an awful hole in my lawn.
4. It was a big, light gray automobile.
5. I had my first bad accident on Main Street.
6. My best black dress is being repaired.
7. We will have a fine new house.
8. My new yellow cotton dress is in the bedroom closet.
9. His music won him four gold records.
10. Your car was hit by a 1983 brown Ford car.

Practice 2
1. —
2. It is not safe to go by an empty house on foot.
3. It was hard to drive on the snowy road.
4. It is good to see you again.
5. It's time to move into my own apartment.
6. It's rude to talk with food in your mouth.
7. It's time for the city to get a better zoo.
8. My mother was glad to see her nieces.
9. These plants are good to eat.
10. We are afraid to go out alone.

Practice 3
Answers will vary.

Practice 4
1. —
2. Paul couldn't see because of the fog.
3. The dog can't run free because of the city law.
4. Paul was unhappy because of the car accident.
5. Duke was so blue because of his report card.
6. Jerry Dawson was angry because of Bob's dog.

Practice 5
1. —
2. Paul could hardly stop his car in time.
3. Jake said hardly anything in answer to Sam's questions.
4. Joe Brunoski could hardly speak any English at first.
5. Jerry Dawson would hardly speak to Bob Shaw.
6. The city council hardly agrees on anything.

Practice 6
1. —
2. Paul could hardly stop his car in time, could he?
3. Jake said hardly anything to Sam, did he?
4. Joe Brunoski hardly spoke any English, did he?
5. Jerry would hardly speak to Bob, would he?
6. The city council hardly agrees on anything, do they?

Practice 7
See page 73 in *Skill Book 4.*

LESSON 13

Practice 1
1. —
2. We call her Kit.
3. We call him Jimmy.
4. We call him Bob.
5. We call him Tommy.
6. We call him Luke.
7. We call her Fran.
8. We call her Liz.
9. We call him Dave.
10. We call her Pam.
11. We call him Jack.
12. We call her Molly.

Practice 2
1. —	
2. will, would	4. will, would
3. will, would	5. will, would

Practice 3
Answers will vary.

Practice 4
1. —	6. up
2. up	7. with
3. out	8. out, out
4. up	9. with
5. out	10. up

Practice 5
Answers should match the sentences read by the teacher.

Practice 6
Jackie Robinson was born in the South in 1919. In 1947, he started playing with the Brooklyn Dodgers baseball team. In 1955, he led the Dodgers to win the World Series. Jackie played with the Dodgers for 10 years. In 1962, he was voted into the Baseball Hall of Fame.

LESSON 14

Practice 1
1. —
2. Didn't you forget something?
3. Wouldn't your family like some fresh fish?
4. Doesn't it feel good to sit down?
5. Isn't he handsome?
6. Doesn't Canada have Thanksgiving Day in October?
7. Wasn't Jackie Robinson the first black player in the major leagues?
8. Don't you like to watch television?
9. Doesn't Jake want to stay in the woods forever?
10. Isn't this the best book you have ever read?

Practice 2
1. —
2. buys, bought, has bought
3. thinks, thought, has thought
4. brings, brought, has brought
5. catches, caught, has caught
6. fight, fought, have fought

Practice 3
A. 1. —
2. Lan ought to thank Tom.
3. Ed ought to get a job.
4. You ought to tie up your dog.
5. Everyone ought to help clean the neighborhood.
6. Gladys ought to run for office.

B. 1. —
2. Tom ought not to be unhappy about winning third prize.
3. Children ought not to play with matches.
4. The city ought not to have a lot of empty houses.
5. Duke ought not to quit school and get a job.
6. You ought not to fly the flag in the rain.

Practice 4
1. —
2. Lewis had a dream as he grew up.
3. Lan's father watched as Tom opened the car door.
4. Lan watched as Tom caught some fish.
5. As Paul was driving along the highway, he saw an accident.
6. As she sat in the car, she had time to think.

Practice 5
1. —
2. Who brought Lan home?
3. What is singing?
4. Who got letters from Viet Nam?
5. What was parked in front of the house?
6. What is behind the door?

LESSON 15

Practice 1
1. —
2. I thought I might get unemployment insurance.
3. I thought I might not come home after work.
4. My friend said the factory might need someone to repair the machines.
5. They said it might rain a lot.
6. Jake said that he might move.
7. I thought I might not have enough money.
8. Roy said he might not be able to buy any toys for his sons for Christmas.
9. Joyce said she might get a job.
10. Jimmy said he might be able to make some money clearing the snow.

Practice 2
1. —
2. telling
3. to phone
4. buying
5. to worry
6. to get
7. repairing, cleaning, and oiling
8. to speak
9. taking
10. to go
11. to clean
12. to annoy
13. to oil and to repair
14. to find
15. slowing (to slow)

Practice 3
1. —
2. unhappy
3. unfurnished
4. unsure
5. untrue
6. unsafe
7. unseen
8. unable
9. unborn
10. unchanged
11. uneaten
12. unhurt
13. unmarked
14. unpainted
15. unrepaired
16. unsaid
17. unspent
18. untested
19. untold
20. unzip

Practice 4
1. —
2. The apartment is unfurnished.
3. The living room was unpainted.
4. She unzipped the jacket.
5. This neighborhood is very unsafe.
6. Why is Duke so unhappy?

Practice 5
1. —
2. I did go to the state employment office.
3. I do want a big, beautiful Christmas tree.
4. Tran Ty Lan did take the tickets.
5. She does get tired from working all day.
6. You do like him a lot.
7. They do try to help every month.
8. I did make a payment on my car loan.
9. You do want to marry again.
10. I do want a job.
11. Jackie did play with the Dodgers for 10 years.
12. It does feel good to sit down.

Practice 6
Answers will vary.

Practice 7
1. the
2. a
3. a
4. a
5. the
6. the
7. the
8. a
9. an

LESSON 16

Practice 1

	Noun	Adj.	Adv.
1.	—		
2.	blindness	blind	blindly
3.	wind	windy	XXX
4.	darkness	dark	darkly
5.	happiness	happy	happily
6.	sickness	sick	sickly
7.	dirt	dirty	XXX
8.	slowness	slow	slowly
9.	lightness	light	lightly
10.	rain	rainy	XXX

Practice 2
1. —
2. quickly
3. cloudy
4. awfully
5. quietly
6. rainy
7. sharply
8. completely
9. windy
10. dirty

Practice 3
Answers without the words in parentheses should be counted as correct, even though they do not use *who* or *which*.
1. —
2. The section of the newspaper which has only ads is the classified ad section.
3. The accident was caused by a truck which was unable to make the sharp turn at the bottom of Hill Street.
4. Two houses (which are) at the corner of Hill St. and Maple Ave. were almost destroyed.
5. The house on Maple Ave., which belongs to Center City Land Company, was empty.
6. Mary Garcia, who lives at 105 Maple Ave., told reporters what she saw.
7. The cat, (which is) a two-year-old female, is free to a good home.
8. Terry's needs a cook, who must be experienced and fast.
(Terry's needs an experienced, fast cook.)

Practice 4
1. —
2. Not only do I clean the machines, but I also oil and repair them.
3. Not only is the news on Channel 3, but it is also on Channel 5 and Channel 9.
4. Not only do unemployed people smoke and drink more, but they also hit their children more.
5. Not only should you talk to your family, but you should also tell the children the truth.
6. Not only did he buy some toys for the children, but he also bought them some clothes.
7. To get an apartment, not only do you have to read the ads, but you also have to make a lot of telephone calls.

Practice 5
Answers will vary.

Practice 6
See page 102 in *Skill Book 4*.

LESSON 17

Practice 1
Answers will vary.

Practice 2
1. —
2. There weren't many passengers on the bus.
3. Tell me where the book is.
4. We have been living in Center City for the last three years.
5. Why don't you throw that rude man off the bus?
6. The bell will ring when the program is ready to begin.
7. Michael went with his mother because he wanted to see the machine shop.
8. The Mitchells heard the bell ring.
9. Some girls don't like chemistry, but I do.

Practice 3
1. —
2. What about baking some cookies?
3. What about asking her younger brother?
4. What about the Mitchell family?
5. What about the open house at school?
6. What about a cup of coffee?

Practice 4
Answers will vary.

Practice 5
1. —
2. He's a a bus driver.
3. She's a school teacher.
4. He's a basketball player.
5. She's a basketball coach.
6. He's a newspaper editor.
7. They are apartment managers.
8. He's a truck driver.
9. They are fire fighters.
10. He's an apple grower.

Practice 6
Answers should match sentences read by the teacher.

Practice 7
Answers will vary.

LESSON 18

Practice 1
1. —
2. How happy Gordon was!
3. How strange the tale was!
4. How gentle Gordon and Gene were!
5. How proud the Chang family was!
6. How hard it was to accept war and killing!

Practice 2
1. —

3. out	5. for
3. up, near	6. out
4. up	7. of

Practice 3
1. —
2. Before Gene went to war, he said good-by to all his friends.
3. After Gordon went into the armed services, he became a medic.
4. After the war was over, the men wanted to go home to their families.
5. You must cool the cookies for a few minutes before you remove them from the pan.
6. After Chris had chorus practice at 6:30, she would meet her parents at 7:30.
7. After we ate dinner, we went into the living room to watch TV.
8. After class was over, Tom gave Lan a ride home.

Practice 4 and 5
Answers will vary.

Practice 6
1. —
2. The Snack Shop needs a cook who is experienced.
3. Mrs. King, whose son is a farmer, teaches school.
4. Not only did I bake a cake but I also made coffee.
5. I didn't go to school because of my cold.
6. What about baking some cookies?
7. How happy Gordon was!
8. Lan should thank Tom.
9. He went into the living room because he wanted to watch TV.
10. Although I had a bad cold, I went to work.

Practice 7
See page 115 in *Skill Book 4*.

LESSON 19

Practice 1

1. —	5. She's Mexican.
2. He's African.	6. He's Chinese.
3. She's Asian.	7. He's Cuban.
4. She's Canadian.	8. He's Indian.

Practice 2
1. —
2. The better you speak English, the more other people understand you.
3. The more you read, the more you learn.
4. The bigger the car, the better.
5. The bigger the headline, the bigger the news story.
6. The more people there are at the party, the better it is.
7. The faster you do your homework, the sooner you will watch TV.

Practice 3
1. A. —
   B. Asian elephants are smaller than African elephants.
2. A. African elephants have more knobs on their trunk than Asian elephants do.
   B. Asian elephants have fewer knobs on their trunk than African elephants do.
3. A. African elephants are harder to train than Asian elephants are.
   B. Asian elephants are easier to train than African elephants are.
4. A. Ginger spent more money than Kitty did.
   B. Kitty spent less money than Ginger did.
5. A. Ginger weighs more than Kitty does.
   B. Kitty weighs less than Ginger does.
6. A. Ginger is older than Kitty is.
   B. Kitty is younger than Ginger is.

Practice 4
Answers will vary.

Practice 5

1. —	6. because
2. As (When)	7. so
3. where	8. If (When)
4. When	9. When (If)
5. although	10. so

Practice 6
Ann has given two English books to Ed. He knows he has to give the two books back to her after he finishes reading them. Ed wants to read the books and to have his two sons read them, too. He knows they will learn a lot of things from reading the books and asking questions about them.

Practice 7
1. —
2. Elephants can be trained to do many things.
3. Elephants are used as work animals.
4. Elephant tusks can be sold for a lot of money.
5. Elephants are still being killed although there are laws against such killings.
6. Elephants have been trained to work in shows.

Practice 8
Answers will vary.

LESSON 20

Practice 1
Answers will vary.

Practice 2

1. —	6. On, in
2. in, in	7. at
3. on	8. on
4. at	9. at
5. in	10. at

Practice 3
1. —
2. This is the sixth accident there in two years.
3. Don't avoid telling people you are out of work.
4. I have been living here for the last three months.
5. Don't give up looking for a job.
6. I will help you if you need help.
7. She was disappointed in me.
8. The other students began to arrive for class.
9. Which U. S. president was born on February 22?
10. People who get a newspaper mainly for sports turn to the sports section first.

Practice 4
A. 1. Rent.
   2. 5%.
   3. 6%.
   4. Education.
   5. Transportation.
   6. Just about right.
   7. No, he isn't.

B. Answers will vary.
C. Answers will vary.

Practice 5
Answers should match sentences read by the teacher.

LESSON 21

Practice 1
1. —
2. —
3. Indian River Fruit Store — 2
4. The York Street Pet Shop — 3
5. Ann's Hat Shop — 1
6. The Pizza Place — 2
7. Valley Utility Company — 3
8. Lake Charlotte High School — 2
9. The Bakery — 1
10. Chang's Asian Food Shop — 1

Practice 2
1. —
2. Ms. Judy Chan
3. Dr. Ann Fisher
4. Mr. Ned Johnson
5. Mr. Carlos Lopez
6. Mr. Fred Miller
7. Ms. Molly Smith

Practice 3
1. —
2. What does *weekly* mean?
   Weekly means once every seven days.
3. What does *guide* mean?
   Guide means to point out the way.
4. What does *improve* mean?
   Improve means to get better.
5. What does *speed* mean?
   Speed means how fast something goes.
6. What does *physician* mean?
   Physician means medical doctor.

Practice 4

	Noun	Adj.	Adv.
1.	—	—	—
2.	health	healthy	healthily
3.	sadness	sad	sadly
4.	safety	safe	safely
5.	fairness	fair	fairly
6.	poor	poor	poorly
7.	snow	snowy	XXX
8.	gladness	glad	gladly
9.	openness	open	openly
10.	pain	painful	painfully

Practice 5
1. —
2. Whose medicine is on the table?
3. Whose family did Tom give some fish to?
4. Whose car got hit from behind?
5. Whose book is this?
6. Whose mother is in the hospital?

Practice 6
1. —
2. The days are getting longer and longer.
3. She said his name over and over.
4. I read the letter again and again.
5. I'm feeling better and better every day.
6. Today more and more people are learning to use computers.

Practice 7
1. —
2. to
3. too
4. to, too
5. too, to
6. two, to
7. To, to

Practice 8
Answers should match sentences read by the teacher.

LESSON 22

Practice 1
1. —
2. He's a factory worker.
3. He's a cancer researcher.
4. She's a high school student.
5. She's a newspaper reporter.
6. She's a dog trainer.
7. They are home owners.
8. They are tree growers.
9. He's a cotton farmer.
10. She's a college teacher.

Practice 2
1. —
2. there
3. Their
4. They're
5. They're, there
6. They're
7. their
8. there

Practice 3
1. —
2. takes
3. take
4. did
5. made
6. takes

Practice 4
1. —
2. At each town, the people came out to cheer him.
3. As Terry ran into Ontario, he got weaker and weaker.
4. Terry's Marathon of Hope was still inspiring all of Canada.
5. Sometimes, people joined Terry and ran a few miles with him to cheer him on.
6. He told funny stories when friends came to visit.

Practice 5
1. —
2. Jake will never move out of the woods.
3. The neighbors are proud of their clean parks.
4. It's not safe to play with matches.
5. Sam has a fine new watch.
6. Paul could hardly see the road, could he?
7. Didn't you forget something?
8. Tom caught a cold last week.
9. She's great. (One possible answer)

Practice 6
George Carver was born in 1864. He lived with the Carvers on their farm. When George was about 12, he left the farm to go to school. When he was 22, he graduated with honors from high school. He wanted to go to college but had to wait three years. First he went to Simpson College and later to Iowa State University.

LESSON 23

Practice 1
Answers may vary. Typical answers are given.
1. —
2. No, it is not permitted. Wear something else.
3. No, it is not permitted. Eat in the kitchen.
4. No, you must not. It's not safe.
5. No, it is not permitted. It's not safe.
6. No, you must not. This is a business phone.
7. No, it is not permitted. Call your doctor for a prescription.
8. No, you must not. The fire department needs to use the fire lanes.
9. No, it is not permitted. Those places must be kept open for the handicapped.

Practice 2
In 1803, President Thomas Jefferson bought the Louisiana Territory from the French. It was a huge, wild country. Jefferson picked Lewis and Clark to explore the territory. They left St. Louis in May of 1804 and started up the Missouri River. Sacajawea was their guide. They did not see the Pacific Ocean until Nov. 7, 1805.

Practice 3
1. —
2. Unless we have a guide, we will never reach the Pacific Ocean.
3. Captain Lewis would not hire Charbonneau unless Sacajawea, his wife, went along.
4. The Shoshonis would not have welcomed Lewis and Clark unless Sacajawea was with them.
5. The men on the expedition would die unless they ate the horses.

Practice 4
Illiterates, Frank Laubach, Asia, Africa, North America, South America, Europe, Dr. Laubach, He, Several, *Life*

Practice 5
1. —
2. Lewis and Clark were heroes when they got back to St. Louis.
3. Some people claim that she died in 1812 in her twenties.
4. The hardest part of the journey came in the next two months.
5. No other American woman has been honored by so many statues.

Practice 6
1. an
2. in
3. the
4. for
5. the
6. for
7. for
8. the
9. for
10. the
11. the
12. of
13. a
14. in

Practice 7
See *People and Places*, pages 45-46.

Word List

Page	Lesson & Practice	Word
23	3-8	between
23	3-8	change
23	3-8	mail
23	3-8	*new
23	3-8	postal
23	3-8	postage
29	5-2	ambulance
29	5-2	company
29	5-2	hospital
29	5-2	insurance
29	5-2	library
48	9-3	candy
48	9-3	outlet
48	9-3	restroom
48	9-3	shoe
48	9-3	sweet
48	9-3	video
53	10-1	schedule
56	10-6	lottery
69	13-1	Edward
69	13-1	Elizabeth
69	13-1	Frances
69	13-1	Pamela
85	16-5	additional
88	17-2	correct
104	20-4	expense
104	20-4	% (per cent)
107	21-1	central
107	21-1	modern
107	21-1	pizza
116	23-1	elevator
116	23-1	jeans
116	23-1	lane

*Indicates a sight word.